Date: 8/24/17

641.86 SIN
Sinclair, Mima.
Rainbow bakes :40 show-
stopping sweet treats /

PALM BEACH COUNTY
LIBRARY SYSTEM
3650 Summit Boulevard
West Palm Beach, FL 33406-4198

RAINBOW BAKES
40 SHOW-STOPPING SWEET TREATS

Mima Sinclair

Photography by Danielle Wood

Mima Sinclair is a food writer who has cooked, tested, written, and developed recipes for numerous cookbooks and food magazines and worked with a number of top chefs. This is her third book with Kyle Books, following the bestselling **Mug Cakes** and **Gingerbread Wonderland**, which have sold over half a million copies worldwide!

KYLE BOOKS

For my sisters Linsey, Storm, Amber, and Sarah.

When you unleash a child in the kitchen with food coloring, a bake just isn't as gratifying without it. To this day I still can't understand why Dad turned down slices of our psychedelic rainbow masterpieces!

Published in 2017 by Kyle Books
www.kylebooks.com

Distributed by National Book Network
4501 Forbes Blvd, Suite 200,
Lanham, MD 20706
Phone: (800) 462-6420
Fax: (800) 338-4550
customercare@nbnbooks.com

First published in Great Britain in 2016 by
Kyle Books, an imprint of Kyle Cathie Ltd

10 9 8 7 6 5 4 3 2 1

ISBN 978-1-909487-60-4

Text © 2016 Mima Sinclair
Design © 2016 Kyle Books
Photography © 2016 Danielle Wood

Mima Sinclair is hereby identified as the author
of this work in accordance with Section 77 of the
Copyright, Designs, and Patents Act 1988.

All rights reserved. No reproduction, copy, or
transmission of this publication may be made
without written permission. No paragraph of
this publication may be reproduced, copied, or
transmitted save with written permission or in
accordance with the provisions of the Copyright
Act 1956 (as amended). Any person who does any
unauthorized act in relation to this publication may
be liable to criminal prosecution and civil claims
for damages.

Designer: Louise Leffler
Photographer: Danielle Wood
Illustrator: Sarah Leuzzi
Food Stylist: Mima Sinclair
Props Stylists: Lauren Miller and Lydia Brun
Project Editor: Sophie Allen
Editorial Assistant: Hannah Coughlin
Editorial Adaptation: Abi Waters
Production: Nic Jones, Gemma John and
Lisa Pinnell

Library of Congress Control Number: 2016956950

Color reproduction by ALTA London
Printed and bound in China by 1010
International Printing Ltd.

CONTENTS

INTRODUCTION

You know how you have always been told not to play with your food? Well forget it all! I give you permission to paint your kitchen and your food with the colors of the rainbow.

Adding a little color pop to your baking is a fantastic way to show personality and style in the most delicious way possible. Whether you want jaws to drop when your cake is revealed, to hear a chorus of "ooh" when you slice into it, or to be asked "how did you do that!?" Now is the time to get color obsessed—I promise your cake stand and cookie jar will never be the same again.

Vibrant and playful recipes have become so popular in recent years that since the explosion of the first rainbow cake it seems we can't get enough of eye-popping layered baked goods, brightly swirled bagels, and even rainbow grilled cheese! When people see their first rainbow cake it mentally goes down on their baking bucket list! And I have a few more to add to your must bake-and-devour list, so whether you're after a tiny rainbow treat or an indulgent six-layered extravaganza, you've come to the right place.

Baking can be a lot of fun and experimenting in the kitchen can lead to incredible creations to show off to friends and family. What isn't so fun is when it goes wrong and you can't work out why. The two common factors that can cause a rainbow meltdown are food coloring and sprinkles, but fear not, I've included some great tips to make sure your rainbows come out perfectly.

So what are you waiting for? Taste the rainbow today!

TIPS & TECHNIQUES

RAINBOW SPRINKLES

There are so many different rainbow sprinkles available the main problem is trying to not buy all of them!

Nonpareils/hundreds and thousands—tiny spherical balls

Jumbo sprinkles—a larger version of nonpareils

Vermicelli/strands—small strands

Jimmies—a large thicker version of vermicelli

Confetti—small flat round discs

SPRINKLES FOR DECORATING

You can use whatever takes your fancy! There are no rules here, just have fun.

SPRINKLES FOR BAKING

Before you embark on a confetti baking extravaganza please take note. It might seem like a simple task—just fold through some rainbow sprinkles and voilà! However, not all rainbow sprinkles can withstand the baking process.

Firstly, the best and brightest results come from artificially colored sprinkles, their naturally colored sprinkle counterparts struggle to be bright enough and loose their color while baking.

Secondly, you must use nice big, fat rainbow sprinkles, also known as jimmies or confetti sprinkles. Buy the most vibrant color selection you can find as they will produce the most impressive rainbow flecks in your bakes. Any kind of nonpareils tend to be too small and the color will be lost long before the bake is out of the oven.

FOOD COLORING

Liquid food coloring used to be the only choice available but now we are spoiled for choice with pastes, gels, and powdered versions. However, these can all create dramatically different outcomes. I like to use gels and pastes, because they produce vibrant colors and you only require a small amount. Good brands to look out for are Wilton, Sugarflair, and Americolor. I find that some of the liquid colorings can require a large volume to reach my desired shade and therefore can upset the liquid content of my batter. They can also have an odd flavor that lingers even after baking.

LIQUID

These water-based dyes are readily available in the baking aisle of almost all grocery stores. They tend to come in little bottles that allow you to drip the dye, drop by drop, into your mixture. They are the least intense so can be good for pastel shades, but when you require a bolder tone these dyes can let you down. You can end up using a significant amount to try to achieve your desired color, so much so that the extra liquid can upset the ingredient ratios.

Good for—icing and pastel cake

GEL

These thick gel-type liquids are available in the baking aisle of large grocery stores, cook shops or online. They typically come in small squeezy bottles that allow you to drop a drip at a time into your mixture. The color is more concentrated than the liquid coloring so a smaller amount will impart a more vivid color, great when you want to minimize the amount of liquid added.

Good for—icing, cake, and dough

PASTE

A very thick, super concentrated version of a gel color, these are available in cooking stores and online. These pastes come in little pots and you can dip a toothpick or knife tip in to scoop out the tiniest bit of paste. A very small amount will produce a lovely intense, saturated color. Great for recipes where minimal liquid is desired. These pastes do, however, require more mixing to blend the color to avoid a marbled, uneven effect, which can cause over-mixing in certain recipes i.e. cookies and doughs.

Good for—confectionery, icing, and cake

POWDER

A powder form of food dye. Trickier to get hold of but available in some cooking shops and online. It comes in small pots and this dry mix is ideal for coloring when no moisture is desired. It can be difficult to combine into thick doughs or batters but very successful for coloring baked goods where sensitivity to liquid is high.

Good for—macarons & meringues

NATURAL FOOD COLORING

A water-based color derived from natural and plant sources i.e. turmeric and beet. They come in little bottles that allow you to drip the dye, drop by drop, into your mixture. These are healthier than the synthetic colorings. Available in health food stores they will achieve muted shades, but will struggle with the vibrant tones required to make rainbow layer cakes.

Good for—allergy sufferers

WHOLE CAKES

RAINBOW CAKE

SERVES 18   PREP TIME: 1½ HOURS, PLUS COOLING, CHILLING, AND SETTING   COOK TIME: 40 TO 50 MINUTES

There is nothing quite as spectacular as a classic rainbow cake.

27oz/3¼ cups/6¾ sticks unsalted butter, softened
26oz/3¾ cups superfine sugar
9 large eggs, lightly beaten
26oz/5⅔ cups self-rising flour, sifted
1 teaspoon fine salt
3fl oz/generous ⅓ cup whole milk
2 teaspoons vanilla extract
food coloring pastes (purple, blue, green, yellow, orange, and pink)

FOR THE CREAM CHEESE ICING

28oz/3½ cups/7 sticks unsalted butter, softened
35oz/7 cups powdered sugar, sifted
28oz/3½ cups full-fat cream cheese
1 teaspoon vanilla extract

TO DECORATE

1oz rainbow confetti sprinkles
2 candy necklaces
2 wooden skewers

MAKE EDIBLE BUNTING TO DECORATE YOUR CAKE BY TYING A CANDY NECKLACE TO SKEWERS.

1. Preheat the oven to 350°F. Grease and line three 8-inch round cake pans with parchment paper.

2. Using an electric hand mixer, beat the butter and superfine sugar together in a large bowl until light and fluffy. Gradually add the eggs, beating well after each addition. Sift in the flour and salt and fold through evenly with a large spoon. Stir in the milk and vanilla extract until combined.

3. Weigh the mixture, divide it between six bowls. Add a different food coloring paste to each bowl, until you reach your required colors. Spoon three of the cake mixtures into the pans, spreading evenly. Bake for 20 to 25 minutes, or until a skewer inserted into the center comes out clean. Let cool for 5 minutes, then turn out onto a wire rack and let cool completely. Wash and dry, then re-grease and line the cake pans. Bake the remaining colored cake mixtures and cool as before.

4. Once the cake layers are cold, use a serrated knife to trim the tops to make the cakes level, then trim the cake edges (using an upturned plate that is just smaller than the cake, as a guide).

5. For the cream cheese icing, beat the butter and powdered sugar together in a bowl until light and fluffy. Gradually beat in the cream cheese, a spoonful at a time, then beat in the vanilla extract until smooth and combined. Sandwich the cake layers together, spreading a few tablespoons of the icing between each layer, starting with the purple layer, then the blue, green, yellow, orange, and pink ones. Cover the cake completely with a thin layer of icing to catch all the crumbs, then chill in the refrigerator for 1 hour.

6. Thickly spread the remaining icing over the cake to cover it, then use an offset spatula or icing scraper to create a lovely flat top and sides. Stick rainbow confetti to the bottom half of the cake, tapering them off as you go up. Let set in the refrigerator for 1 hour, then remove the cake 20 minutes before serving.

PIÑATA CAKE

SERVES 18   PREP TIME: 1¼ HOURS, PLUS COOLING   COOK TIME: 20 TO 25 MINUTES

The ultimate party centerpiece—one slice of this impressive cake will reveal its hidden sweet secret! Choose your own color icing and type of candies.

12oz/1½ cups/3 sticks unsalted butter, softened, plus extra for greasing
12oz/1¾ cups superfine sugar
6 large eggs
12oz/2⅔ cups all-purpose flour
2½ teaspoons baking powder
1 teaspoon fine salt
1 teaspoon vanilla extract
4 tablespoons whole milk

FOR THE BUTTERCREAM
18oz/2¼ cups/4½ sticks unsalted butter, softened
35oz/7 to 7¼ cups powdered sugar, sifted
1 teaspoon vanilla extract
pink food coloring paste
(or your chosen color)

TO DECORATE
35oz colorful mixed candies

YOU WILL NEED
round cookie cutter, about 4 inches diameter

1. Preheat the oven to 350°F. Grease and line three 8-inch round cake pans with parchment paper.

2. Using an electric hand mixer, beat the butter and superfine sugar together in a large bowl until light and fluffy. Add the eggs, one at a time, beating well after each addition. Sift in the flour, baking powder, and salt and fold through evenly with a large spoon. Stir in the vanilla extract and milk until combined.

3. Divide the mixture between the prepared pans, spreading evenly. Bake for 20 to 25 minutes, or until a skewer inserted into the center comes out clean. Let cool in the pans for 5 minutes, then turn out onto a wire rack and let cool completely.

4. Meanwhile, for the buttercream, beat the butter, powdered sugar, and vanilla extract together in a bowl until light and fluffy. Stir in pink food coloring paste, until you reach your required color.

5. Once the cake layers are cold, take one layer and cut a hole out of the center using the cookie cutter. Repeat with a second cake layer. Sandwich these two layers together with some pink buttercream, then cover the top layer with more buttercream. Fill the central hole with mixed candies, then place the final uncut cake layer on top to enclose the candies completely.

6. Use the remaining buttercream to cover the cake completely, then gradually (without eating too many!) cover the whole cake with the remaining mixed candies.

HIDDEN CENTER LOAF CAKE

SERVES 10   PREP TIME: 1¼ HOURS, PLUS COOLING, FREEZING, AND SETTING   COOK TIME: 2 HOURS 20 MINUTES

The gorgeous paint-like dribbles on this cake and the hidden rainbow center
will have people squealing!

FOR THE HIDDEN NUMBER CUT-OUTS

7oz/generous ¾ cup/1¾ sticks
   unsalted butter, softened,
   plus extra for greasing
7oz/1 cup superfine sugar
3 large eggs
7oz/1½ cups self-rising flour
¼ teaspoon fine salt
1 teaspoon vanilla extract
3 tablespoons whole milk
food coloring pastes (purple,
   blue, green, orange, and pink)

FOR THE VANILLA CAKE

11½oz/1½ cups/3 sticks unsalted
   butter, softened
11½oz/1½ cups superfine sugar
5 large eggs
11½oz/2½ cups self-rising flour
½ teaspoon fine salt
1 teaspoon vanilla extract
5 tablespoons whole milk

FOR THE DRIBBLE ICING

7oz/scant 1½ cups royal icing mix,
   sifted
food coloring pastes (blue, green,
   yellow, orange, and pink)

YOU WILL NEED

6 disposable pastry bags (1 large)
cookie cutter number or shape,
   about 12.5 × 15 inch

1. Preheat the oven to 350°F. Grease and line an 8½ × 4½ × 2½-inch loaf pan with parchment paper.

2. For the hidden number cut-outs, using an electric hand mixer, beat the butter and superfine sugar together in a large bowl until light and fluffy. Add the eggs, one at a time, beating well after each addition. Sift in the flour and salt and fold through evenly with a large spoon. Stir in the vanilla extract and milk until combined.

3. Divide the mixture between five bowls and stir a little food coloring paste into each portion, then spoon each into a separate pastry bag and snip a ¼-inch hole off the tips. Pipe the colored cake mixtures into the prepared loaf pan, alternating the colors as you go to create a crazy marbled effect. Tap the pan on the surface to remove any air bubbles.

4. Bake for 1 hour to 1 hour 10 minutes, or until a skewer inserted into the center comes out clean. Let cool in the pan for 10 minutes, then turn out onto a wire rack and let cool completely.

5. Cut the cold loaf cake into 1 inch-thick slices. Use your chosen cutter to cut out the number or shape from each slice, then lay the cut-outs on a baking sheet. Place the sheet in the freezer for 15 minutes while you make the vanilla cake. Save the cake scraps for making cake pops.

6. Preheat the oven again to 350°F. Wash and dry, then re-grease and line the loaf pan. Make the vanilla cake mixture following the instructions given above in step 2. Pour half of the cake mixture into the base of the prepared loaf pan, then spoon the remaining mixture into the large pastry bag and snip a 1-inch hole off the tip.

7. Position the frozen cake cut-outs upright (and close together) in a single row down the center of the pan. Mark the front of your pan with a piece of tape if you are using a number cut-out (so you cut the correct end to reveal forward-facing numbers, for serving). Pipe the remaining vanilla cake mixture around the cut-outs and all over the top to cover them completely, ensuring you fill in any small holes. Smooth the top with the back of a spoon.

8. Bake for 1 hour to 1 hour 10 minutes as above, then turn out and cool as before. Keep track of the marked end of the cake, so you know which end of the cake to slice into to have the forward-facing numbers.

9. For the icing, place the royal icing mix in a bowl and add 2 teaspoons cold water. Stir until smooth, then add a little extra water until you have a thick but just runny icing. Divide between five small bowls and stir a little food coloring paste into each portion.

10. Once the cake is cold, spoon alternate blobs of icing onto the top of the cake, encouraging them to dribble down the sides. If your icing is too thick, add a drop more water; if it is too runny, add a spoonful of extra icing mix.

11. Let set at room temperature for 4 hours before slicing and serving.

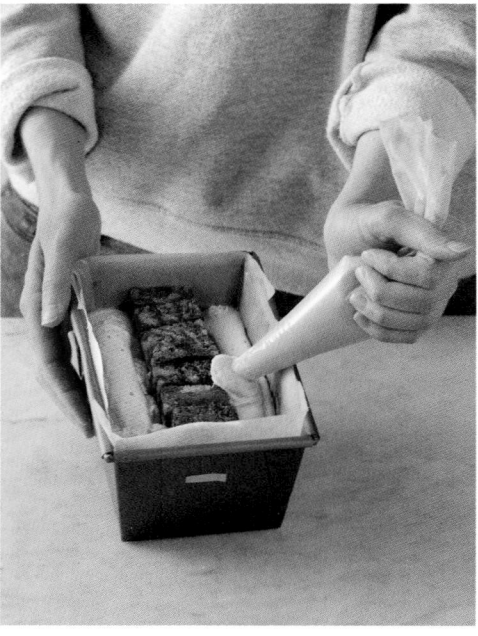

CONFETTI CAKE

SERVES 16   PREP TIME: 50 MINUTES, PLUS COOLING AND CHILLING   COOK TIME: 20 MINUTES

What is the secret to a successful confetti cake? Big, fat rainbow sprinkles, that's what! Their smaller brothers and sisters simply won't do the job.

9oz/1 cup/2¼ sticks unsalted butter, softened, plus extra for greasing
9oz/1¼ cups superfine sugar
4 large eggs
9oz/generous 1¾ cups all-purpose flour
2 teaspoons baking powder
1 teaspoon fine salt
1 teaspoon vanilla extract
3 tablespoons whole milk
3½oz rainbow jimmies (a large thicker version of vermicelli) —I use Wilton's

FOR THE BUTTERCREAM

14oz/1¾ cups/3½ sticks unsalted butter, softened
1¾lbs/5¾ cups powdered sugar, sifted
1 teaspoon vanilla extract

TO DECORATE

10½oz rainbow sprinkles (nonpareils/hundreds and thousands)

1. Preheat the oven to 350°F. Grease and line three 7-inch round cake pans with parchment paper.

2. Using an electric hand mixer, beat the butter and superfine sugar together in a large bowl until light and fluffy. Add the eggs, one at a time, beating well after each addition. Sift in the flour, baking powder, and salt and fold through evenly with a large spoon. Stir in the vanilla extract and milk until combined, then fold in the sprinkles until evenly dispersed.

3. Divide the mixture between the prepared pans, spreading evenly. Bake for 20 minutes, or until a skewer inserted into the center comes out clean. Let cool in the pans for 5 minutes, then turn out onto a wire rack and let cool completely.

4. Meanwhile, for the buttercream, beat the butter, powdered sugar, and vanilla extract together in a bowl until light and fluffy. Once the cake layers are cold, sandwich them together with some of the buttercream, then coat the cake completely with the remaining buttercream. Chill in the refrigerator for 1 hour.

5. To decorate, pour the rainbow sprinkles into a large baking sheet. Carefully lift the cake and roll it through the sprinkles, pressing them into the buttercream and using your hands to gently press them into the top of the cake. Slice and serve.

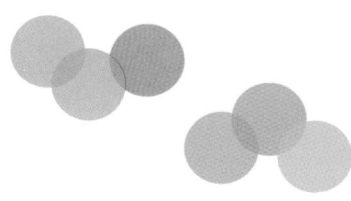

NAKED RAINBOW TIER

SERVES 16   PREP TIME: 40 MINUTES, PLUS COOKING   COOK TIME: 20 TO 25 MINUTES

After baking a rainbow, a naked cake is the perfect way to show it off.

5⅔oz/¾ cup/1½ sticks unsalted butter, softened, plus extra

14oz/2 cups superfine sugar

5 large egg whites

1½ teaspoons vanilla extract

4oz sour cream

13¼oz/2¾ cups all-purpose flour

1 tablespoon baking powder

1 teaspoon baking soda

½ teaspoon fine salt

8fl oz/1 cup whole milk

food coloring pastes (purple, blue, green, yellow, orange, and red)

FOR THE CREAM CHEESE ICING

9oz/1 cup/2¼ sticks unsalted butter, softened

12oz/2½ cups powdered sugar, sifted

9oz/1 cup full-fat cream cheese

1 teaspoon vanilla extract

YOU WILL NEED

1 disposable pastry bag

CREATING A TIERED EFFECT CAN BE A SIMPLE BUT VISUALLY EXCITING WAY TO LAYER YOUR CAKE

1. Preheat the oven to 350°F. Grease and line three 8-inch cake pans and three 7-inch cake pans with parchment paper.

2. Using an electric hand mixer, beat the butter and superfine sugar together in a large bowl until light and fluffy. Add the egg whites, one at a time, beating well after each addition. Lightly beat in the vanilla extract and sour cream. Sift the flour, baking powder, baking soda, and salt into a bowl, then add to the egg white mixture in three batches, alternating with the milk. Fold through evenly with a large spoon.

3. Divide the mixture between six smaller bowls. Take a rounded tablespoon each from three of the bowls and add to each of the other bowls. Add a little purple, blue, and green food coloring paste to the fuller bowls and yellow, orange, and red coloring paste to the smaller bowls, mixing until combined.

4. Spoon the purple, blue, and green mixtures into the 8-inch cake pans, spreading evenly. Bake for 10 to 12 minutes, or until a skewer inserted into the center comes out clean. Let cool for 5 minutes, then turn out onto a wire rack and let cool completely. Spoon the yellow, orange, and red mixtures into the 7-inch cake pans, then bake and cool as above.

6. Once the cake layers are cold, using a serrated knife, carefully trim the crusts off the edges of the cakes. Use the base of a slightly smaller cake pan or an upturned plate to cut around.

7. For the icing, beat the butter and powdered sugar together in a bowl until light and fluffy. Gradually beat in the cream cheese, a spoonful at a time, then the vanilla extract. Spoon one-third of the icing into the pastry bag, then snip a ½-inch hole off the tip. Pipe a circle of icing around the inner edge of the purple layer, then fill in the center with a few tablespoons and spread evenly. Top with the blue layer and then repeat with the remaining icing, leaving the top of the cake un-iced.

ANTI-GRAVITY CAKE

SERVES 18   PREP TIME: 1½ HOURS, PLUS COOLING, SETTING, AND CHILLING   COOK TIME: 20 TO 25 MINUTES

Watch kids and adults have their minds blown with this edible illusion—the anti-gravity cake, which is great for themed party centerpieces!

12oz/1½ cups/3 sticks unsalted butter, softened, plus extra for greasing

12oz/1¾ cups superfine sugar

6 large eggs

12oz/2⅔ cups all-purpose flour

2½ teaspoons baking powder

1 teaspoon fine salt

1 teaspoon vanilla extract

4 tablespoons whole milk

FOR THE BUTTERCREAM

18oz/2¼ cups/4½ sticks unsalted butter, softened

35oz/7 cups powdered sugar, sifted

2 teaspoons vanilla extract

food coloring (pink and blue)

FOR THE DRIBBLE ICING

3½oz/¾ cup royal icing mix, sifted

food coloring pastes (yellow and purple)

TO DECORATE

1oz white chocolate (minimum 30% cocoa solids), melted

3½oz rainbow sprinkles

YOU WILL NEED

1 thick wooden skewer

pastry bag fitted with a large closed star tip

small clear plastic pot

1. Preheat the oven to 350°F. Grease and line three 8-inch round cake pans with parchment paper.

2. Using an electric hand mixer, beat the butter and superfine sugar together in a large bowl until light and fluffy. Add the eggs, one at a time, beating well after each addition. Sift in the flour, baking powder, and salt and fold through evenly with a large spoon. Stir in the vanilla extract and milk until combined.

3. Divide the mixture between the prepared pans, spreading evenly. Bake for 20 to 25 minutes, or until a skewer inserted into the center comes out clean. Let cool in the pans for 5 minutes, then turn out onto a wire rack and let cool completely.

4. Meanwhile, for the buttercream, beat the butter, powdered sugar, and vanilla extract together in a bowl until light and fluffy. Spoon a sixth of the buttercream into a separate bowl, then stir in a little pink food coloring paste and set aside. Add blue food coloring paste to the remaining buttercream.

5. Once cold, cut each cake in half horizontally. Sandwich the cake layers together with some of the blue buttercream and then coat the cake completely with the remainder.

6. For the dribble icing, place the royal icing mix in a bowl and add 2 teaspoons cold water. Stir until smooth, then add a little extra water until you have a thick but just runny icing. Divide between two small bowls and stir a little yellow food coloring paste into one portion and purple into the other.

7. Spoon a trail of yellow icing around the top edge of the cake, encouraging a little dribble down the sides. Let set for 30 minutes, then repeat with the purple icing. Leave for a further 30 minutes to set.

ONCE YOU MASTER THE TECHNIQUE, YOU CAN SUSPEND ALL YOUR FAVORITE TREATS ABOVE THE CAKE!

8. Meanwhile, for the decoration, using a small paintbrush, brush two-thirds of a thick wooden skewer in the melted white chocolate, then coat in rainbow sprinkles. Place in the refrigerator to set hard.

9. Once the dribble icing has set, spoon the pink buttercream into the pastry bag, then pipe small stars around the top edge of the cake. Take your sprinkle-coated skewer and insert into the center of the cake, pushing it in at an angle until the uncovered wooden end is no longer visible (just the sprinkle-coated part is visible). Pour a pile of the rainbow sprinkles around the base of the skewer and press them in lightly.

10. Put the remaining rainbow sprinkles into the small clear pot and cover the top neatly with plastic wrap to stop all the sprinkles from falling out. Carefully pierce one corner of the pot, then carefully insert the top end of the sprinkle-coated skewer into it, so it hooks into the neck and the pot balances. If the pot is too heavy, remove some of the sprinkles so it is able to balance. Add other decorations, such as a unicorn, if liked, pressing down slightly into the icing to secure. Serve and watch the wonderment on your guest's faces!

FIREWORKS CHOCOLATE CAKE

SERVES 16   PREP TIME: 1¼ HOURS, PLUS COOLING   COOK TIME: 20 MINS

This decadent chocolate cake is the perfect celebration for July 4th or New Year's Eve. Take a slice to reveal bright neon buttercream within!

2¾oz/¾ cup cocoa powder
5 large eggs
1 teaspoon vanilla extract
10½oz/2¼ cups self-rising flour
2 teaspoons baking powder
14oz/2 cups superfine sugar
2fl oz/scant ¼ cup sunflower oil
9oz/1 cup/2¼ sticks unsalted butter,
   softened, plus extra for greasing

FOR THE BUTTERCREAM

9oz/1 cup/2¼ sticks unsalted butter,
   softened
18oz/3½ cups powdered sugar, sifted
1 teaspoon vanilla extract
food coloring pastes (as below)

FOR THE CHOCOLATE GANACHE

8½fl oz/generous 1 cup heavy cream
3 tablespoons superfine sugar
14oz dark chocolate (minimum
   70% cocoa solids), finely chopped

TO DECORATE

2¾oz/½ cup powdered sugar
neon food coloring pastes
   (teal, purple, orange, magenta)
1 tablespoon white sprinkles/
   nonpareils

YOU WILL NEED

fine paintbrush and sparkler
   fountain or indoor sparklers

1. Preheat the oven to 350°F. Grease and line four 7-inch round cake pans and line with parchment paper.

2. Put the cocoa in a bowl and stir in 7fl oz/generous ¾ cup boiling water until smooth, then set aside to cool slightly. Put the eggs, vanilla extract, and 3fl oz/⅓ cup cold water in a bowl and whisk together until combined. Set aside.

3. In a large bowl, sift the flour, baking powder, and sugar. Add the cocoa mixture, oil, and butter. Beat together for 1 minute using an electric hand mixer, then gradually add the egg mixture, beating well after each addition. Divide the mixture between the pans, spreading evenly. Bake for 20 minutes, or until a skewer inserted into the center comes out clean. Let cool in the pans for 10 minutes, then turn out onto a wire rack and let cool fully.

4. Meanwhile, for the buttercream, beat the butter, powdered sugar, and vanilla together in a bowl until light and fluffy. Divide between three smaller bowls and color each portion with teal, purple or orange food coloring paste. Once the cake layers are cold, sandwich them together with the colored buttercreams, spreading a different colored one between each layer.

5. For the ganache, place the cream and sugar in a non-stick saucepan. Bring just to a boil, then remove from the heat and add the chocolate. Leave for 2 minutes before gently stirring until smooth and glossy. Let cool and thicken slightly before spreading over the cake with an offset spatula.

6. To decorate, mix the powdered sugar with a few drops of cold water until you have a thick but still runny icing. Divide between four small bowls and add food coloring paste to each. Using a fine paintbrush, paint fireworks onto the cake and decorate with the white sprinkles. Let set in the refrigerator for 30 minutes before decorating with indoor sparklers.

RED VELVET RAINBOW CAKE

SERVES 10   PREP TIME: 1½ HOURS, PLUS COOLING   COOK TIME: 40 MINS

The hypnotic rows of rainbow-colored candies on this cake will have
the kids mesmerized.

4oz/½ cup/1⅛ sticks unsalted butter,
   softened, plus extra for greasing
10½oz/1½ cups superfine sugar
2 large eggs
1½oz/scant ½ cup cocoa powder
1 to 2 teaspoons red food
   coloring paste
1 teaspoon vanilla extract
8fl oz/1 cup buttermilk
10½oz/2¼ cups all-purpose flour
1 teaspoon baking soda
½ teaspoon fine salt
1 tablespoon white wine vinegar

CREAM CHEESE BUTTERCREAM

7oz/¾ cup/1¾ sticks unsalted butter,
   softened
9oz/1¾ cups powdered sugar
7oz/scant 1 cup full-fat cream cheese
½ teaspoon vanilla extract

TO DECORATE

1¾lbs mixed Original and Tropical
   Skittles or rainbow-colored
   candies

1. Preheat the oven to 350°F. Grease a 9 × 3-inch bundt pan or ring mold.

2. Using an electric hand mixer, beat the butter and superfine sugar together in a medium bowl until light and fluffy. Add the eggs, one at a time, beating well after each addition. In a small bowl, combine the cocoa, food coloring paste, and vanilla extract to make a thick paste. Whisk this into the butter mixture.

3. Beat in half the buttermilk until smooth and combined. Sift over the flour, baking soda, and salt and fold through evenly with a large spoon. Gently beat in the remaining buttermilk with the vinegar, then beat the whole mixture for 2 minutes.

4. Pour into the prepared bundt pan, spreading evenly. Bake for 40 minutes, or until a skewer inserted into the center comes out clean. Let cool in the pan for 10 minutes, then turn out onto a wire rack and let cool completely.

5. For the cream cheese icing, beat the butter and powdered sugar together in a bowl until light and fluffy. Gradually beat in the cream cheese, a spoonful at a time, then beat in the vanilla extract until smooth and combined.

6. Once the cake is cold, use a serrated knife to trim the base then cut it in half vertically so you have two crescents. Use some of the cream cheese icing to sandwich the flat sides of the trimmed base together and then "stand" them up on a serving plate or board securing them with a little icing underneath so the cake is the shape of a rainbow.

7. Using an offset spatula, cover the outside of the cake evenly with the remaining icing, then press the Skittles or candies in colored rows over the cake to look like a rainbow.

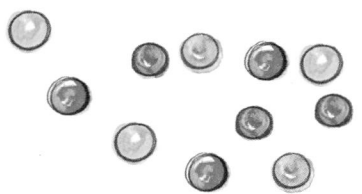

PETAL CAKE

SERVES 18   PREP TIME: 1¼ HOURS, PLUS COOLING AND CHILLING   COOK TIME: 20 TO 25 MINUTES

Before you say "this one's too hard I can't make it" think again. This gorgeous petal effect is much simpler to achieve than you'd imagine.

12oz/1½ cups/3 sticks unsalted butter, softened, plus extra for greasing
12oz/1¾ cups superfine sugar
6 large eggs
12oz/2⅔ cups all-purpose flour
2½ teaspoons baking powder
1 teaspoon fine salt
1 teaspoon vanilla extract
4 tablespoons whole milk

FOR THE BUTTERCREAM

27oz/3¼ cups/6¾ sticks unsalted butter, softened
53oz/10½ cups powdered sugar, sifted
1 teaspoon vanilla extract
food coloring pastes (purple, blue, green, yellow, orange, and pink)

YOU WILL NEED

ruler
toothpick
6 disposable pastry bags

1. Preheat the oven to 350°F. Grease and line three 8-inch round cake pans with parchment paper.

2. Using an electric hand mixer, beat the butter and superfine sugar together in a large bowl until light and fluffy. Add the eggs, one at a time, beating well after each addition. Sift in the flour, baking powder, and salt and fold through evenly with a large spoon. Stir in the vanilla extract and milk until combined.

3. Divide the mixture between the prepared pans, spreading evenly. Bake for 20 to 25 minutes, or until a skewer inserted into the center comes out clean. Let cool in the pans for 5 minutes, then turn out onto a wire rack and let cool completely before cutting each cake in half horizontally.

4. Meanwhile, for the buttercream, beat the butter, powdered sugar, and vanilla extract together in a large bowl until light and fluffy. Divide between six smaller bowls and color each portion with a different food coloring paste. Once the cake layers are cold, sandwich them together using a few tablespoons of each different colored buttercream between each layer, then coat the cake completely with a thin layer of yellow buttercream to catch all the crumbs.

5. Using a ruler, measure the height of your cake, then using a toothpick, mark the mid-height point all the way round. Chill the cake in the refrigerator for 1 hour.

6. Spoon each of the remaining colored buttercreams into a separate pastry bag and snip ½-inch holes off the tips. Line up the bags in the order in which you want to pipe the colors, then using the marked center guideline, pipe rows of dots onto the cake—three above the line and three below. Then, use the

I USED AMERICOLOR "ELECTRIC"
GELS TO ACHIEVE THESE GORGEOUS
BRIGHT SHADES.

back of a teaspoon to spread each dot of icing from the center to the right. Clean the spoon between each use.

7. Continue with your next row of dots, but move the colors all down one position, checking often to make sure your lines are vertical. Continue in this way with all the remaining colored buttercreams but don't spread the final row of dots.

8. Pipe a circle of dots around the outer top edge of the cake. Spread these dots as before, then continue to the center, reducing the amount of dots when it gets tight. Finish with one dot in the center.

POLKA DOT SURPRISE BUNDT CAKE

SERVES 14 PREP TIME: 1¼ HOURS, PLUS COOLING AND FREEZING COOK TIME: 1½ HOURS

This cake is so impressive, but is secretly really rather easy to make. Topped with its cheerful rainbow icing, you are bound to get plenty of smiles from your guests.

FOR THE RAINBOW CAKE BALLS

4oz/½ cup/1⅛ sticks unsalted butter, softened, plus extra for greasing
4oz/scant ⅔ cup superfine sugar
2 large eggs
4oz/1 cup self-rising flour
1 teaspoon lemon or orange extract
food coloring pastes (purple, blue, green, yellow, orange, and red)

FOR THE VANILLA CAKE

9¾oz/1¼ cups/2½ sticks unsalted butter, softened
9¾oz/1⅓ cups superfine sugar
4 large eggs
9¾oz/2 cups self-rising flour
½ teaspoon fine salt
1 teaspoon vanilla extract
3 tablespoons whole milk

cont. overleaf

1. Preheat the oven to 350°F. Lightly grease the cake pop mold.

2. For the rainbow cake balls, using an electric hand mixer, beat the butter and superfine sugar together in a medium bowl until light and fluffy. Add the eggs, one at a time, beating well after each addition. Sift in the flour and fold through evenly with a large spoon. Stir in the lemon or orange extract until combined.

3. Divide the mixture between six bowls and stir a little food coloring paste into each portion. Place the base of the mold on a baking sheet. Carefully spoon some of the colored batters into each hole of the prepared mold, filling each one right to the top so it rises and fills the other half of the mold during baking. Gently place the lid of the mold (with the air holes on the top) in position and secure in place.

4. Bake for 12 to 14 minutes. Insert a toothpick into a hole to check if the cakes are cooked—it should come out clean. Remove the lid and let cool in the mold for 10 minutes, then gently press the cakes out of the mold onto a wire rack and let cool completely.

5. Quickly wash and dry the mold, lightly grease again and spoon in the remaining cake mixtures (the mixture should make about 26 cake balls in total). Repeat the baking and cooling as before. Once cold, trim off any excess cake from the balls and place them on a baking sheet in the freezer for 30 minutes.

FOR THE BUTTERCREAM

3½oz white chocolate (minimum
    30% cocoa solids), roughly
    chopped
5½oz/⅔ cup/1¼ sticks unsalted
    butter, softened
5½oz/1 cup powdered sugar, sifted
1 teaspoon vanilla extract
food coloring pastes (purple, blue,
    green, yellow, orange, and pink)

YOU WILL NEED

20-hole/cup cake pop molds
6 disposable pastry bags,
    each fitted with a different
    shaped tip

● ● ● ● ● ● ● ● ● ● ● ● ● ●

**IF YOU DON'T HAVE A CAKE POP MOLD,
INSTEAD YOU CAN MAKE AND BAKE
THE CAKE BALL MIXTURE IN A GREASED
AND LINED 8-INCH ROUND CAKE
PAN (BAKE IT FOR ABOUT
15 MINUTES, THEN TURN OUT AND
LET COOL). ONCE COLD (IDEALLY
24 HOURS LATER), BREAK THE CAKE
INTO PIECES AND DIVIDE BETWEEN SIX
SMALL BOWLS. PULSE EACH BATCH IN A
FOOD-PROCESSOR WITH 1 TABLESPOON
OF THE UNCOLORED BUTTERCREAM
AND A LITTLE FOOD COLORING PASTE.
ROLL INTO BALLS AND FREEZE BEFORE
BAKING IN THE CAKE.**

● ● ● ● ● ● ● ● ● ● ● ● ● ●

6. Preheat the oven again to 350°F. Grease a 9 × 3-inch bundt pan
    or ring mold. For the vanilla cake, using an electric hand mixer,
    beat the butter and superfine sugar together in a medium bowl
    until light and fluffy. Add the eggs, one at a time, beating well
    after each addition. Sift in the flour and salt then fold through
    evenly with a large spoon. Gently stir in the vanilla extract and
    milk until combined.

7. Spoon a small amount of cake mixture into the prepared pan,
    spreading evenly. Drop a few cake balls into the mixture, then
    cover with more cake mixture. Continue layering the cake balls
    and cake mixture until you have used them all up, finishing with
    a layer of cake mixture spread evenly.

8. Bake for 1 hour, or until a skewer inserted into the center
    comes out clean. Cover the cake with foil after 30 minutes
    if it's browning too quickly. Let cool completely in the pan
    before turning out onto a plate.

9. For the buttercream, melt the chocolate in a heatproof bowl
    over a pan of barely simmering water. Let cool slightly. Beat the
    butter and powdered sugar together in a separate bowl until
    creamy, then beat in the melted chocolate and vanilla extract
    until combined.

10. Divide the buttercream between six smaller bowls and stir
    a little food coloring paste into each portion. Spoon each
    colored buttercream into a pastry bag and then randomly
    pipe colored swirls over the top of the cake. Slice to reveal
    the surprise inside and serve.

VERTICAL OMBRE CAKE

SERVES 20   PREP TIME: 2¼ HOURS, PLUS COOLING   COOK TIME: 1½ HOURS

A real show stopper, which requires a little more effort, but don't be put off!
It is well worth it for the deliciously light cake and truly fluffy buttercream.

FOR THE JELLY ROLL SPONGE CAKES

5⅔oz/¾ cup/1½ sticks salted butter,
    melted, plus extra for greasing
16 large eggs
14oz/2 cups superfine sugar,
    plus extra for sprinkling
21oz/4½ cups all-purpose flour
3 teaspoons baking powder
peach food coloring paste

FOR THE ROUND SPONGE CAKES

6 large eggs
5½oz/¾ cup superfine sugar,
    plus extra for sprinkling
8oz/1¾ cups all-purpose flour
1 teaspoon baking powder
2oz/¼ cup/½ stick salted butter,
    melted

FOR THE BUTTERCREAM

6 large egg whites
12oz/1¾ cups superfine sugar
18oz/2½ cups/4½ sticks unsalted
    butter, softened, cut into cubes
1 teaspoon vanilla extract
peach food coloring paste

YOU WILL NEED

candy thermometer
large palette knife
organic fresh flowers, to decorate

1. Preheat the oven to 350°F. Grease and line a 10 × 15-inch jelly roll pan with parchment paper.

2. For the jelly roll sponge cakes, using an electric hand mixer, whisk 4 eggs and 3½oz/½ cup of the sugar together in a medium, grease-free bowl until pale, thick, and doubled in volume. Sift 5½oz/generous 1 cup of the flour and ¾ teaspoon of the baking powder over the egg mixture, then pour 1½oz melted butter down the side of the bowl. Using a large metal spoon, very gently fold in until just combined, being careful not to knock the air out.

3. Pour the mixture into your lined pan and gently smooth with an offset spatula. Bake for 12 to 14 minutes, or until springy and dry to the touch.

4. Place a large sheet of parchment paper onto a clean surface and sprinkle with the extra superfine sugar. Carefully turn out the hot sponge cake onto the paper, peeling away the lining paper. Loosely roll up the cake from a short side, with the sugared paper inside, then let cool completely on a wire rack.

5. Repeat the steps above three more times (to make four jelly roll sponge cakes in total), but each time adding a little peach food coloring paste to the cake mixture, making each one slightly darker than the previous one.

6. For the round sponge cakes, grease and line two 9-inch round cake pans with parchment paper. Repeat step 2 above using all the ingredients listed on the left. Divide this mixture between the prepared pans, spreading evenly, then bake for 12 to 14 minutes, or until springy and dry to the touch. Turn out onto sugared paper and let cool completely on a wire rack.

7. While all the cakes cool, make the Swiss meringue buttercream. Place the egg whites and sugar into a medium, heatproof

I'VE USED A PRETTY PASTEL FOOD COLORING PASTE BUT THIS CAKE ALSO LOOKS GREAT WITH A PUNCHIER GREEN OR BLUE OMBRE EFFECT.

bowl over a pan of simmering water. Whisk constantly until the mixture reaches 158°F on a candy thermometer and the sugar is completely dissolved, about 10 to 15 minutes.

8. Transfer to a large bowl, then using an electric hand mixer, whisk for about 10 minutes, or until firm peaks form and the mixture has almost cooled to room temperature. Gradually add the butter, one cube at a time, beating well between additions, until all the butter is combined and the mixture is pale and smooth. Whisk in the vanilla extract.

9. Take one-third of the mixture and place it in a bowl. Divide the remaining buttercream evenly between three separate bowls. Add a little food coloring paste to these three bowls, making each buttercream slightly darker than the previous one.

10. Place a round cake on your cake stand and spread with a thin layer of the plain buttercream. Set aside. Carefully unroll the sheet cakes and use a knife to cut each one in half lengthwise. Spread one half of the lightest sheet cake with a thin layer of plain buttercream, then roll up tightly (minus the paper this time) to create a log. Place the rolled cake upright in the center of the round cake on the cake stand. You will only need one of the palest sheet cake halves, so discard the other (or use it to make a trifle or similar).

11. Take the next palest sheet cake half and spread thinly with the next shade of buttercream. Roll around the plain cake, starting from where the first cake ended (so joining them together). Continue with the remaining sheet cake halves, spreading them with buttercream and then rolling each one around the other, graduating from light to dark cakes. Spread a little plain buttercream over the top of the rolled cakes. Then top with your final round cake. Trim your round cakes to fit the rolled cakes.

12. Spread any remaining plain buttercream over the top of the cake, then gradually spread the lightest peach buttercream over the top third of the cake, spread the next shade over the middle third of the cake, then finally, spread the darkest shade over the lower third of the cake. Use a long palette knife to gently blend the colors together. Decorate with fresh flowers and serve.

RAINBOW YULE LOG

SERVES 8   PREP TIME: 45 MINUTES, PLUS COOLING   COOK TIME: 12 TO 14 MINUTES

Break from tradition and serve the brightest, most beautiful
Christmas Yule log anyone has ever seen!

1½oz/3 tablespoons unsalted
butter, melted and cooled,
plus extra for greasing
4 large eggs
3½oz/½ cup superfine sugar,
plus extra for sprinkling
food coloring pastes (purple, blue,
green, yellow, orange, and red)
5½oz/generous 1 cup all-purpose
flour
¾ teaspoon baking powder

FOR THE WHIPPED CREAM FILLING

9fl oz/generous 1 cup whipping
cream
1¾oz/generous ⅓ cup powdered
sugar, plus extra for dusting
½ teaspoon vanilla extract

YOU WILL NEED

6 disposable pastry bags
a clean dish towel

1. Preheat the oven to 350°F. Grease and line a 10 × 15-inch jelly
roll pan with parchment paper.

2. Using an electric hand mixer, whisk the eggs and superfine sugar
together in a medium bowl until pale, thick, and doubled in
volume. Working quickly, gently divide the mixture between six
smaller bowls and stir a food coloring paste into each portion.

3. Sift the flour and baking powder into a separate bowl to
combine evenly. Sprinkle 3 tablespoons of the flour mixture
over each portion of colored egg mixture with a drizzle of the
melted butter, then fold it in very gently with a metal spoon
until just combined, being careful not to knock the air out.

4. Gently spoon each colored mixture into a separate pastry
bag, then cut off each tip to create a ¾-inch hole. Pipe lines
of the mixtures diagonally across the prepared pan in a
rainbow pattern, making sure the lines touch each other, and
continuing until the pan is full and all the mixture is used up.
Bake for 12 to 14 minutes, or until springy and dry to the touch.

5. Place a large sheet of parchment paper onto a clean surface
and sprinkle with superfine sugar. Carefully turn out the hot
cake onto the paper, peeling away the lining paper. Loosely roll
up the cake from a short side, with the sugared paper inside,
wrap with a damp dish towel, then let cool completely on a
wire rack.

6. For the whipped cream filling, pour the cream into a large
bowl and, using an electric hand mixer, whip the cream until
soft peaks form. Sift over the powdered sugar and add the
vanilla extract, then whisk again briefly until just combined.

7. Gently unroll the sponge cake and spread evenly with the cream
filling. Re-roll the cake (minus the paper), finishing with the join
underneath. Dust with powdered sugar before serving.

SMALL BAKES

OVER THE RAINBOW CUPCAKES

MAKES 12   PREP TIME: 40 MINUTES, PLUS COOLING   COOK TIME: 20 MINUTES

Find your pot of gold at the end of the rainbow with these delightful multi-colored rainbow layered cupcakes.

6oz/¾ cup/1½ sticks unsalted
   butter, softened
6oz/generous ¾ cup superfine sugar
3 large eggs
6oz/1⅓ cups self-rising flour
½ teaspoon fine salt
1 teaspoon vanilla extract
2 tablespoons whole milk
food coloring pastes (purple, blue,
   green, yellow, orange, and red)

FOR THE ICING

5½oz/⅔ cup/1¼ sticks unsalted
   butter, softened
10½oz/2 cups powdered sugar, sifted
7oz white marshmallow fluff

TO DECORATE

6 rainbow fizzy belt candies, halved
edible gold dust

YOU WILL NEED

12 paper liners
disposable pastry bag fitted with
   a ½-inch round tip

1. Preheat the oven to 350°F. Line a 12-hole muffin pan with paper liners.

2. Using an electric hand mixer, beat the butter and superfine sugar together in a medium bowl until light and fluffy. Add the eggs, one at a time, beating well after each addition. Sift in the flour and salt and fold through evenly with a large spoon. Stir in the vanilla extract and milk until combined.

3. Divide the mixture between six bowls. Stir a little food coloring paste into each portion. Divide the purple cake mixture between the paper liners and spread evenly. Top this with the blue cake mixture, spreading evenly on top. Continue in this way with the remaining cake mixtures (green, yellow, orange, then red), so that you end up with rainbow layers in each cupcake case.

4. Bake for 20 minutes, or until the cakes are risen and spring back when lightly pressed. Let cool in the pan for 5 minutes, then transfer to a wire rack and let cool completely.

5. Meanwhile, for the icing, beat the butter and powdered sugar together in a bowl until light and fluffy. Add the marshmallow fluff and beat until smooth and combined.

6. Once the cupcakes are cold, spoon the icing into the pastry bag and pipe swirls of icing onto each cupcake. Decorate with the rainbow belts and gold dust just before serving.

RAINBOW TOWERS

MAKES 15   PREP TIME: 1 HOUR, PLUS COOLING AND CHILLING   COOK TIME: 30 TO 45 MINUTES

Layers of rainbow cake are sandwiched together, then cut into squares.
Perfect for an afternoon treat and a nice change from the classic cupcake.

26oz/3¼ cups/6¾ sticks unsalted
butter, softened, plus extra for
greasing
26oz/3¾ cups superfine sugar
9 large eggs, lightly beaten
26oz/5⅔ cups self-rising flour
1 teaspoon fine salt
3fl oz/⅓ cup whole milk
2 teaspoons vanilla extract
food coloring pastes (purple, blue,
green, yellow, orange, and red)

FOR THE CREAM CHEESE ICING

10½oz/1⅓ cups/2¾ sticks unsalted
butter, softened
13¼oz/2⅔ cups powdered sugar,
sifted
10½oz full-fat cream cheese
1 teaspoon vanilla extract

1. Preheat the oven to 350°F. Grease and line two 10 × 15-inch
jelly roll pans with parchment paper.

2. Using an electric hand mixer, beat the butter and superfine
sugar together in a large bowl until light and fluffy. Gradually
add the eggs, beating well after each addition. Sift in the flour
and salt and fold through evenly with a large spoon. Stir in the
milk and vanilla extract until combined.

3. Weigh the mixture, then divide it evenly between six smaller
bowls. Add a different food coloring paste to each bowl, adding
a little at a time and stirring until you reach your required
colors. Spoon two of the colored cake mixtures into the
prepared pans, spreading evenly.

4. Bake for 10 to 15 minutes, or until a skewer inserted into the
center comes out clean. Let cool in the pans for 5 minutes,
then turn out onto wire racks and let cool completely. Quickly
wash and dry, then re-grease and line the pans. Spoon two
more of the colored cake mixtures into the pans and spread
evenly, then bake and cool as before. Repeat this step one final
time to bake the final two cakes.

5. While the cakes are cooling, make the cream cheese icing.
Beat the butter and powdered sugar together in a bowl until
light and fluffy. Gradually beat in the cream cheese, a spoonful
at a time, then beat in the vanilla extract until smooth and
combined.

6. Once all the cakes are cold, sandwich the cakes together with a
layer of icing between each one, starting with the purple one,
then the blue, green, yellow, orange, and red ones. Chill in the
refrigerator for 1 hour.

7. Use a serrated knife to trim the edges and then cut the cake
into 15 squares to serve.

RAINBOW CAKE IN A JAR

SERVES 1   PREP TIME: 20 MINUTES, PLUS COOLING   COOK TIME: 20 TO 25 MINUTES

This one is for when it's just you and you can't trust yourself with a whole cake in the house! Baked individually in a jar, it's soon ready to enjoy and there's no need to share it.

2¾oz/⅓ cup/¾ stick unsalted butter, softened, plus extra for greasing
2¾oz/⅓ cup superfine sugar
1 large egg
2¾oz/½ cup self-rising flour
pinch of fine salt
¼ teaspoon vanilla extract
food coloring pastes (purple, blue, green, yellow, orange, and red)

FOR THE ICING

1¾fl oz/scant ¼ cup heavy cream
1 teaspoon powdered sugar, sifted
¼ teaspoon vanilla extract
1 teaspoon edible confetti or rainbow sprinkles

YOU WILL NEED

1 × 14fl oz ovenproof glass jar

1. Preheat the oven to 350°F and grease a jar with butter.

2. Using an electric hand mixer, beat the butter and superfine sugar together in a medium bowl until light and fluffy. Add the egg, beating well, then sift in the flour and salt and fold through evenly with a spoon. Stir in the vanilla extract until combined.

3. Divide the mixture between six small bowls. Stir a little food coloring paste into each portion. Spoon the colored cake mixtures into the prepared jar, spooning them one on top of the other and working your way through the rainbow—purple, blue, green, yellow, orange, and red.

4. Bake for 20 to 25 minutes, or until a skewer inserted into the center comes out clean. Set the jar aside to cool completely.

5. For the icing, whip the cream, powdered sugar and vanilla extract together in a small bowl until soft peaks form. Once the cake is cold, spoon the icing over the cake and scatter with edible confetti or rainbow sprinkles before serving.

PASTEL CUPCAKES

MAKES 12   PREP TIME: 25 MINUTES, PLUS COOLING   COOK TIME: 20 MINUTES

Bite into these playful cupcakes, topped with a dreamy pastel icing,
to reveal the swirl of rainbow colors inside.

8oz/1 cup/2 sticks unsalted butter,
  softened
8oz/generous 1 cup superfine sugar
zest of 1 orange
zest of 1 lemon
3 large eggs
8oz/1¾ cups all-purpose flour
1½ teaspoons baking powder
½ teaspoon fine salt
1 teaspoon orange extract
food coloring pastes (blue, green,
  yellow, and pink)

FOR THE BUTTERCREAM

9oz/generous 1 cup/2¼ sticks
  unsalted butter, softened
1lb 2oz/3⅔ cups powdered sugar,
  sifted
food coloring pastes (as above)

YOU WILL NEED

12 paper cupcake liners
large pastry bag fitted with an
  open star tip

1. Preheat the oven to 350°F. Line a 12-hole muffin pan with paper liners.

2. Using an electric hand mixer, beat the butter and superfine sugar together in a medium bowl until light and fluffy. Beat in the citrus zests, then add the eggs, one at a time, beating well after each addition. Sift in the flour, baking powder, and salt and fold through evenly with a large spoon. Stir in the orange extract until combined.

3. Divide the mixture between four bowls. Stir a little food coloring paste into each portion. Place spoonfuls of the colored mixtures randomly into the cupcake cases, then gently drag a skewer through the mixture two or three times to give a marbled effect.

4. Bake for 20 minutes until the cakes are risen and spring back when lightly pressed. Let cool in the pan for 5 minutes, then transfer to a wire rack and let cool completely.

5. For the buttercream, beat the butter and powdered sugar together in a medium bowl until light and fluffy. Divide between four smaller bowls and color each portion with a different food coloring paste.

6. Take the pastry bag and roll it down halfway. Add a spoonful of one of the four colored buttercreams to the bottom of the bag, making sure you leave space for the three others by its side—as you want all the colors to pipe out at the same time. Add a spoonful of the second colored buttercream, alongside the first, trying to push the icing down to the same point in the bag as the first. Repeat with the third and fourth colors, filling the bottom of the bag. Continue adding the buttercream colors in the same places (placing each layer

of four buttercreams on top of the previous one), avoiding creating air pockets, until the bag is three-quarters full and all the buttercream is used up. Roll up the rest of the bag and twist the top to secure.

7. Once the cupcakes are cold, pipe some buttercream on top of each cupcake in a spiral pattern, working from the outside edge inward and keeping constant pressure on the icing bag. Continue the spiral pattern, into a second layer of icing on top of the first working gradually towards the center. To finish, release the pressure on the bag, press down lightly then pull straight up to get a nice finish.

SPRINKLE WITH EDIBLE GLITTER FOR AN EVEN MORE MAGICAL FEEL.

EASTER EGG CAKE POPS

MAKES 30   PREP TIME: 1¼ HOURS, PLUS COOLING, FREEZING, CHILLING, AND SETTING   COOK TIME: 20 MINUTES

Take a break from all the chocolate at Easter and enjoy some delicious vanilla-speckled egg cake pops instead!

9oz/generous 1 cup/2¼ sticks
  unsalted butter, softened,
  plus extra for greasing
9oz/1¼ cups superfine sugar
4 large eggs
9oz/1¾ cups self-rising flour
½ teaspoon fine salt
1 teaspoon vanilla extract
2 tablespoons whole milk

FOR THE BUTTERCREAM

5½oz/⅔ cup/1¼ sticks unsalted
  butter
10½oz/generous 2 cups powdered
  sugar, sifted

TO DECORATE

2¼lbs colored candy melts (7oz of
  each color in blue, green, yellow,
  orange, and pink)
2 vanilla beans, split in half
  lengthwise and seeds scraped out
2½ teaspoons vegetable oil
  (optional)

YOU WILL NEED

30 long lollipop sticks
cake pop stand (or a Styrofoam
  block to stand the cake pops up
  in when they are decorated)

1. Preheat the oven to 350°F. Grease and line two 8-inch round cake pans with parchment paper.

2. Using an electric hand mixer, beat the butter and superfine sugar together in a large bowl until light and fluffy. Add the eggs, one at a time, beating well after each addition. Sift in the flour and salt and fold through evenly with a large spoon. Stir in the vanilla extract and milk until combined.

3. Divide the mixture between the prepared pans, spreading evenly. Bake for 20 minutes, or until a skewer inserted into the center comes out clean. Let cool in the pans for 5 minutes, then turn out onto a wire rack and let cool completely.

4. Meanwhile, to make the buttercream, whisk the butter and powdered sugar together with an electric mixer until light and fluffy.

5. Once the cakes are cold, finely crumble them into a large bowl and then stir through the buttercream, mixing until well combined. Taking small portions—about a heaped tablespoonful of the mixture—roll each portion into an egg shape, making 30 eggs in total. Place on a tray and freeze for about 15 minutes until firm but not frozen, then transfer all the cake pops to the refrigerator so they stay chilled.

6. Place one batch (one color) of the colored candy melts in a medium heatproof bowl set over a small saucepan of barely simmering water. Make sure the water doesn't touch the base of the bowl and be careful not to overheat the candy melts as they can burn easily. Add one-fifth of the vanilla seeds and then stir occasionally until the mixture is melted and smooth—if it is a little thick, add ½ teaspoon vegetable oil to make it more fluid.

7. Take six cake pops out of the refrigerator. Dip a lollipop stick into the melted icing, then push it about 1 inch into a cake pop. Dip the entire cake pop into the icing, turning to coat it all over. Try to do this in one motion, because if you keep re-dipping the cake pop, it may come off the stick. Gently rotate the lollipop stick to allow excess icing to drip off, then stick the cake pop into the stand or Styrofoam block. Repeat with the remaining five cake pops and melted icing.

8. Repeat steps 5 and 6 above for each batch of colored candy melts and each batch of six cake pops, melting each icing separately and coating the cake pops with the icing. Let the cake pops set completely before serving.

GLAZED DONUTS

MAKES 16   PREP TIME: 50 MINUTES, PLUS RISING, PROVING, AND COOLING   COOK TIME: 20 TO 25 MINUTES

These donuts are light and chewy and guaranteed to get even
the laziest person out of bed at the weekend!

1lb 2oz/3⅔ cups white bread flour,
   plus extra for dusting
1¾oz/¼ cup superfine sugar
1 teaspoon fine salt
3½oz/½ cup/1 stick unsalted butter,
   chilled and cubed
¼oz packet active dried yeast
5½fl oz/⅔ cup hand-hot water
2 large eggs, lightly beaten
1 quart/33¾fl oz sunflower oil for
   deep-frying, plus extra for greasing

TO DECORATE
14oz/3 cups powdered sugar
food coloring pastes (blue, green,
   yellow, orange, pink, and red)

YOU WILL NEED
1¼-inch round cookie cutter
candy thermometer

> DEEP-FRY THE CENTER CUT-OUTS
> FROM THE DONUTS IN THE HOT OIL
> FOR 1 TO 2 MINUTES, THEN DRAIN
> AND SERVE WARM OR COLD,
> TOSSED IN EXTRA SUPERFINE
> SUGAR, IF YOU LIKE.

1. Lightly grease a large bowl and grease two baking sheets. Sift the flour, sugar, and salt into a large bowl and then using your fingertips, rub in the butter until the mixture resembles breadcrumbs. Fold through the dried yeast.

2. Pour over the warm water and mix until combined. Then add the eggs and mix with a wooden spoon until the mixture forms a dough. Turn out onto a lightly floured surface and knead for 10 minutes by hand (or alternatively, use a stand mixer fitted with a dough hook) until the dough springs back when pressed.

3. Place the dough in the greased bowl and cover loosely with oiled plastic wrap. Let rise in a warm place for 1 to 2 hours, or until doubled in size.

4. Knock the air out of the risen dough by kneading it for 2 minutes on a floured surface. Divide the dough into 16 equal pieces, then shape each one into a smooth ball (do this by rolling each one on the surface with the palm of your hand). Place the dough balls on the prepared baking sheets, leaving room for them to expand as they prove. Cover loosely with oiled plastic wrap and let prove in a warm place for a further 1 hour, or until doubled in size.

5. Lightly oil the cookie cutter and use it to stamp out the middle of each donut. Discard the centers or see Cook's Tips, left, for how to make mini donuts from the centers!

6. Pour the sunflower oil into a large, deep saucepan and heat the oil to 325°F, using the thermometer to check it's hot enough. Drop two or three donuts into the oil, one at a time, and deep-fry on each side for 2 to 3 minutes, or until golden-brown. Remove with a slotted spoon and place on a plate lined with kitchen paper to soak up the excess oil. Repeat with the

● ● ● ● ● ● ● ● ● ● ● ● ● ● ●

**FOR A HEALTHIER ALTERNATIVE BAKE
YOUR DONUTS. FOLLOW STEPS 1 TO 5 ON
THE PREVIOUS PAGE. PREHEAT THE OVEN
TO 350°F AND PLACE THE DONUTS ON A
GREASED BAKING SHEET. BAKE FOR 8 TO
10 MINUTES UNTIL GOLDEN-BROWN ALL
OVER. CONTINUE WITH STEPS 7 TO 10
RIGHT TO FINISH.**

● ● ● ● ● ● ● ● ● ● ● ● ● ● ●

remaining donuts (ensuring the oil is brought back up to temperature for each batch) until they are all cooked.

7. To make the icing, put the powdered sugar in a bowl and stir in 4 to 5 tablespoons of cold water until smooth—you want a thick but still runny consistency. Divide the mixture into six smaller bowls, then stir a little food coloring paste into each portion.

8. Using a teaspoon, draw a ½-inch thick line of one of the colored icings, onto a plate, just longer than the width of your donuts, then repeat with the remaining colored icings, placing them side by side (with all the lines touching to create a square-ish rainbow). Press the base of one of the cooled donuts into the icing and gently drag and lift to the side. Dragging is important to get the icing to stick to the donut. Dip another donut into the icings in the same way. Set them aside on a serving plate.

9. Repeat with the remaining colored icings and donuts, remembering to refresh your icing lines on the plate after every two donuts.

10. Leave the decorated donuts to set for 30 to 60 minutes somewhere cool (but not the refrigerator). These donuts are best eaten fresh, though you can store them in an airtight container (with wax paper between each layer) for up to 3 days.

FRECKLED CINNAMON ROLLS

MAKES 16   PREP TIME: 40 MINUTES, PLUS RISING AND PROVING   COOK TIME: 15-20 MINUTES

Rainbow strands or jimmies really liven up this classic recipe and these tasty sweet rolls are a real treat for the weekend.

10fl oz/1¼ cups whole milk

6 cardamom pods, husks removed
   and seeds ground

1¾oz/3½ tablespoons butter

1lb/3¼ cups white bread flour,
   plus extra for dusting

¼oz packet active dried yeast

1¾oz/¼ cup superfine sugar

½ teaspoon fine salt

2 large eggs

flavorless oil (such as sunflower),
   for greasing

FOR THE CINNAMON FILLING

3½oz/½ cup/1 stick salted butter,
   softened

3oz/⅓ cup/¾ stick soft light
   brown sugar

1 tablespoon ground cinnamon

zest of 1 orange

2½oz rainbow jimmies (a large
   thicker version of vermicelli—
   I use Wilton's)

FOR THE DRIZZLE ICING AND DECORATION

1¾oz/⅓ cup powdered sugar, sifted

½oz rainbow jimmies

1. Heat the milk in a small saucepan with the ground cardamom seeds. Bring just to a boil, then remove from the heat and stir in the butter until melted. Set aside until the mixture has cooled to lukewarm.

2. Meanwhile, sift the flour, yeast, superfine sugar, and salt into a large bowl. Make a well in the center and mix in 1 egg (reserve the remaining egg for the glaze). Pour the flavored milk into the bowl and stir until it comes together to form a soft, sticky dough.

3. Lightly oil a clean surface with 1 to 2 teaspoons of oil. Turn the dough onto the oiled surface (or alternatively, use a stand mixer fitted with a dough hook) and knead for 10 minutes until it's smooth and springs back a little. The dough will be very sticky to begin with but don't add any extra flour as it will get less sticky as you knead. Transfer the dough to a clean, lightly greased bowl. Cover with a clean dish-towel and let rise in a warm place for 30 minutes, until nearly doubled in size.

4. For the cinnamon filling, beat the butter, sugar, cinnamon, and orange zest together in a bowl until soft and spreadable. Lightly flour a clean surface and dust your hands with flour. Tip out the dough and turn once to lightly coat in the flour, then roll it out into a 14 × 10-inch rectangle, with one of the longer sides closest to you.

5. Using your fingers and an offset spatula, spread the cinnamon mixture over the dough right up to the edges, then scatter over the jimmies. Roll up the dough fairly tightly, starting with the long edge closest to you. Finish with the seam underneath, then cut into 16 even slices.

IF THERE IS NOWHERE WARM TO LEAVE YOUR DOUGH TO RISE AND PROVE, PLACE A BOWL OF BOILING WATER IN THE BASE OF A COLD OVEN AND PLACE THE COVERED DOUGH BOWL AT THE TOP. SHUT THE OVEN DOOR AND LEAVE THE DOUGH TO SLOWLY RISE.

6. Grease a deep, round cake pan, about 12 inches in diameter or a 14 × 10-inch roasting pan. Place the cinnamon buns into the prepared pan, spacing them evenly. Cover with the dish-towel and let prove in a warm place for a further 30 minutes until the buns have puffed up and are now touching each other. Meanwhile, preheat the oven to 350°F.

7. Beat the remaining egg and lightly brush it over the cinnamon buns. Bake for 15 to 20 minutes until golden-brown. Leave in the pan for 10 minutes, then turn out onto a wire rack and let cool completely.

8. To make the drizzle icing, in a small bowl, mix the powdered sugar with 1 to 2 teaspoons cold water, stirring to make a thick but drizzling consistency. Drizzle over the cold buns, then scatter generously with the rainbow jimmies before serving.

MULTI-COLORED BAGELS

MAKES 12 PREP TIME: 1 HOUR, PLUS RISING, PROVING, AND COOLING COOK TIME: 25 MINUTES

Brighten your breakfast table by serving up some of these dreamy bagels that are just bursting with color. Lightly toasted, then spread with confetti cream cheese, you are in for a real treat!

26oz/5⅓ cups white bread flour, plus more for dusting
2 × ¼oz packet active dry yeast
2 teaspoons fine salt
3 tablespoons granulated sugar
18fl oz/2 cups hand-hot water
food coloring pastes (orange, pink, purple, and green)
1 teaspoon vegetable oil

FOR CONFETTI CREAM CHEESE
9¾oz cream cheese
2¾oz/½ cup powdered sugar
2 tablespoons rainbow sprinkles

PACKED IN AN AIRTIGHT CONTAINER (WITH WAX PAPER BETWEEN EACH LAYER), THESE BAGELS WILL KEEP WELL IN A COOL, DRY PLACE FOR UP TO 4 DAYS. ALTERNATIVELY, THEY FREEZE WELL FOR UP TO 3 MONTHS (DEFROST BEFORE SERVING). IF STORING THE BAGELS, SIMPLY MAKE THE CONFETTI CREAM CHEESE JUST BEFORE SERVING.

1. Pour the flour, yeast, salt, and sugar into a large bowl and mix to combine. Pour over the warm water and stir with a wooden spoon until the mixture forms a stiff dough. Turn the dough onto a lightly floured surface (or alternatively, use a stand mixer fitted with a dough hook) and knead for 10 minutes until the dough is no longer sticky, adding a little extra flour if needed.

2. Divide and shape the dough into four even balls and then knead a little food coloring paste into each portion.

3. Use the oil to grease four medium bowls, then place a portion of colored dough in each of them, turning to lightly coat in oil. Cover each bowl with lightly greased plastic wrap and let rise in a warm place for 30 minutes.

4. Lightly grease two or three baking sheets and set aside. Knock back the dough by hitting it with your fist (to knock the air out), then re-roll into balls as before. On a sheet of parchment paper, roll out each ball into a ¾ inch-thick rectangle, about 6 × 12 inches in size. Stack the four colored doughs on top of each other on one of the prepared baking sheets, then lightly cover with greased plastic wrap and let prove in a warm place for a further 30 minutes.

5. Slice the proofed stacked doughs into 12 strips, each about 1 × 6 inches. Twist each strip of dough a little to create a spiral and join the ends together. Repeat with the remaining dough and place on the prepared baking sheets. Cover loosely with the greased plastic wrap, then let prove again for another 30 minutes, or until proofed back into their pre-twist size.

6. Preheat the oven to 400°F. Bring a large saucepan of water to a boil. Working in batches of two or three at a time, cook the bagels in the boiling water for 30 seconds each side, turning once. Remove with a slotted spoon, drain on kitchen paper, then transfer back to the greased baking sheets.

7. Once all the bagels are ready, transfer them to the oven and bake for 16 minutes, turning them over halfway through baking. The bagels should color slightly but not brown. Transfer to a wire rack and let cool completely.

8. For the confetti cream cheese, beat the cream cheese and powdered sugar together in a bowl until smooth. Gently fold in the rainbow sprinkles.

9. Once the bagels are cold, cut each one in half horizontally, then lightly toast and serve spread with the confetti cream cheese.

COOKIES

COOKIE KISSES

MAKES 50   PREP TIME: 45 MINUTES, PLUS CHILLING, COOLING, AND SETTING   COOK TIME: 8 MINUTES

Bag up these colorful iced jewels to give to friends and brighten their day with a little rainbow happiness.

2¾oz/⅓ cup/¾ stick unsalted butter
1oz/2½ tablespoons superfine sugar
½ teaspoon vanilla extract
4oz/generous ¾ cup all-purpose
   flour, plus extra
pinch of fine salt

FOR THE ICING

9oz/1¾ cups royal icing mix
food coloring pastes (purple, blue,
   green, yellow, orange, and pink)

YOU WILL NEED

¾-inch cookie cutter
6 disposable pastry bags
½-inch open star tip

PACKED INTO AN AIRTIGHT
CONTAINER AND STORED IN
A COOL, DRY PLACE, THESE
WILL KEEP WELL FOR UP TO
A MONTH. STACK THEM
CAREFULLY, WITH WAX PAPER
BETWEEN EACH LAYER.

1. Line two or three baking sheets with parchment paper. Set side. Using an electric hand mixer, beat the butter, superfine sugar and vanilla extract together in a medium bowl until just combined. Sift over the flour and salt and stir gently until the mixture comes together to form a dough.

2. Turn out onto a lightly floured surface and roll out to ⅛-inch thickness. Cut out 50 rounds using the cookie cutter (or I use the base of a large piping tip), re-rolling the scraps. Transfer to the baking sheets, then chill in the refrigerator for 20 minutes.

3. Preheat the oven to 350°F. Remove the cookies from the refrigerator and bake for 8 minutes until very lightly golden. Let cool completely on the baking trays.

4. For the icing, sift the royal icing mix into a medium bowl, then add 1 tablespoon cold water. Using an electric hand mixer, gently whisk them together for 2 to 3 minutes until you have a smooth, thick icing (like the consistency of toothpaste!)—add an extra drop or two of water if the icing is too stiff.

5. Divide the icing into six small bowls and stir a little food coloring paste into each one. Fill up one pastry bag, fitted with the star tip, with one color of icing, then pipe stars onto some of the cookies. Clean the tip, insert into a clean pastry bag, then repeat with another colored icing. Repeat this process with the remaining colored icings, so that you end up with cookies decorated with different colored stars. Let set in a cool place for at least 2 hours before serving.

CONFETTI COOKIES WITH MARSHMALLOW BUTTERCREAM

MAKES 20   PREP TIME: 40 MINUTES, PLUS CHILLING AND COOLING   COOK TIME: 12 TO 14 MINUTES

These simple shortbread cookies, sandwiched together with scrumptious marshmallow buttercream are sure to get the party started!

8oz/1 cup/2 sticks unsalted butter, softened, plus extra for greasing
4oz/½ cup superfine sugar
8oz/1¾ cups all-purpose flour, plus extra for dusting
3½oz/1 cup cornstarch
½ teaspoon fine salt
2¾oz rainbow Jimmies

FOR THE MARSHMALLOW BUTTERCREAM

5½oz/⅔ cup/1¼ sticks unsalted butter
10½oz/2 cups powdered sugar
7oz marshmallow fluff
food coloring pastes (purple, blue, green, yellow, orange, pink)

YOU WILL NEED

2-inch round fluted cutter
pastry bag with ½-inch round tip

● ● ● ● ● ● ● ● ● ● ● ● ● ●

THESE FREEZE WELL UNFILLED. STACK AS IN STEP 6 IN AN AIRTIGHT CONTAINER AND FREEZE FOR UP TO 3 MONTHS, DEFROST AT ROOM TEMPERATURE BEFORE SANDWICHING TOGETHER WITH BUTTERCREAM.

● ● ● ● ● ● ● ● ● ● ● ● ● ●

1. Using an electric hand mixer, beat the butter and sugar together in a medium bowl until light and fluffy. Sift over the flour, cornstarch, and salt and beat again until smooth and combined. Fold through the rainbow jimmies, then turn out onto a lightly floured surface and gently knead until you have a soft dough.

2. Using two large sheets of parchment paper, roll out the dough between the sheets to ⅛-inch thickness. Transfer the dough (still between the sheets of paper) to a tray and chill in the refrigerator for 1 hour to firm up.

3. Preheat the oven to 350°F. Line three large baking sheets with parchment paper. Remove the cookie dough from the refrigerator and discard the top sheet of paper. Using the cookie cutter, cut out 40 cookies (re-rolling the scraps) and place them on the prepared sheets.

4. Bake for 12 to 14 minutes until golden brown at the edges. Let cool on the baking sheets for 10 minutes until firm, then transfer to a wire rack and let cool completely.

5. For the buttercream, beat the butter and powdered sugar together in a bowl until light and fluffy. Add the marshmallow fluff and beat until smooth and combined. Divide the mixture between six smaller bowls and add food coloring to each.

6. Spoon the colored buttercreams randomly into the pastry bag. Pipe swirls of marshmallow buttercream onto the base of half the cookies, then sandwich these together with the remaining cookies. Packed in airtight containers they will keep well in a cool, dry place for up to 1 week. Stack them carefully, with wax paper between each layer.

RAINBOW COOKIE POPS

MAKES 40   PREP TIME: 1 HOUR, PLUS CHILLING, COOLING, AND SETTING   COOK TIME: 10 MINUTES

The novelty of eating something off a lollipop stick is something all children seem to adore.

7oz/¾ cup/1¾ sticks unsalted
  butter, softened
7oz/1 cup superfine sugar
zest of 1 orange
1 large egg, lightly beaten
14oz/3 cups all-purpose flour,
  plus extra for dusting

FOR THE ICING
12oz/2½ cups royal icing mix
food color pastes (purple, blue,
  green, orange, yellow, and red)

YOU WILL NEED
7 × 2-inch rainbow cookie cutters
40 paper or wooden lollipop sticks
7 disposable pastry bags
⅛-inch round tip

PACKED INTO AN AIRTIGHT CONTAINER AND STORED IN A COOL, DRY PLACE, THESE COOKIES WILL KEEP WELL FOR UP TO 2 WEEKS. STACK THEM CAREFULLY, WITH WAX PAPER BETWEEN EACH LAYER.

1. Using an electric hand mixer, beat the butter, superfine sugar and orange zest together in a medium bowl until just combined and becoming creamy (don't overwork, otherwise the cookies will spread during baking). Add the egg and beat until combined. Sift in the flour and stir gently until the mixture comes together to form a dough. Shape into a ball, then cut in half and wrap each portion in plastic wrap. Chill in the refrigerator for 1 hour.

2. Line three large baking sheets with parchment paper, then set aside. On a lightly floured surface, roll out the dough to ⅛-inch thickness. Using the cookie cutter, cut out 40 cookies, then transfer them to the prepared baking sheets. Insert a lollipop stick into center of each cookie, making sure it is covered in cookie dough. Chill in the refrigerator again for 30 minutes, or speed things up by chilling them in the freezer for 15 minutes.

3. Meanwhile, preheat the oven to 350°F. Remove the cookies from the refrigerator and bake for 10 minutes until golden-brown at the edges. Cool slightly on the baking sheets, then transfer the cookies to a wire rack and let cool completely.

4. For the icing, sift the royal icing mix into a large bowl. Add 2 teaspoons cold water and, using an electric hand mixer, whisk on a low speed for 3 minutes until you have a smooth icing that holds soft peaks (use a low speed as you don't want to incorporate too much air into the icing). Cover the bowl with a damp cloth or plastic wrap to prevent the icing from drying out.

5. Once the cookies are cold, spoon 5 tablespoons of the icing into a pastry bag fitted with the tip and pipe the outlines of the white clouds onto each cookie. Squeeze any remaining icing from the bag into a bowl and add extra icing so you have about 5 tablespoons of icing. Add a few drops of cold water to make the icing thick but runny enough to smooth into the edges of

the clouds. Spoon back into the used pastry bag and fill in the clouds, smoothing the icing to the edges. Let set hard somewhere cool (but not the refrigerator).

6. Divide the remaining icing into six bowls and stir a little food coloring paste into each portion to make the colors of the rainbow. Make sure the icing is thick enough to pipe and only spread a little. Spoon each colored icing into a pastry bag, then cut off a ⅛-inch tip from each one. First pipe a line of red icing across the top of

each cookie between the clouds. Then, making sure you leave space for the orange line, pipe the yellow line. Leaving space for the green line, pipe the blue line, but remember to also leave space at the base for the purple line. By the time you have piped these three lines onto all the cookies, the first cookies iced will be slightly set, so you can continue and fill in the orange, green, and purple lines. Let set hard somewhere cool for at least 4 hours. Serve the cookie pops in candy jars or in a cake pop stand.

DISCO DIP VALENTINE COOKIES

MAKES 30   PREP TIME: 1 HOUR, PLUS CHILLING AND COOLING   COOK TIME: 10 MINUTES

These cute heart-shaped cookies make a great gift for loved ones.

7oz/¾ cup/1¾ sticks unsalted
  butter, softened
7oz/1 cup superfine sugar
1 vanilla bean, split in half and
  seeds scraped out
1 large egg, lightly beaten
14oz/3 cups all-purpose flour,
  plus extra for dusting

FOR THE ICING

18oz/3½ cups royal icing mix
food coloring pastes (blue, green,
  yellow, orange, and pink)

YOU WILL NEED

3-inch heart cookie cutter
6 disposable pastry bags
⅛-inch fine round tip
3 tablespoons rainbow sprinkles,
  to decorate

**IF YOU WANT TO COOK HALF A
BATCH, FREEZE 1 BALL OF DOUGH,
WRAPPED WITH PLASTIC WRAP,
OR PACK UNCOOKED OR COOKED
COOKIES INTO CONTAINERS AND
FREEZE FOR UP TO 3 MONTHS.
MAKE SURE TO HALVE THE ICING
QUANTITY AS WELL.**

1. Using an electric hand mixer, beat the butter, superfine sugar, and vanilla seeds together in a bowl until just combined and becoming creamy (don't overwork, otherwise the cookies will spread during baking). Add the egg and beat until combined. Sift in the flour and stir gently until the mixture comes together to form a dough. Shape into a ball, then cut in half and wrap each portion in plastic wrap. Chill in the refrigerator for 1 hour.

2. Line two or three large baking sheets with parchment paper, then set aside. On a lightly floured surface, roll out the dough to ⅛-inch thickness. Using the cookie cutter, cut out 30 cookies, then transfer them to the baking sheets. Chill in the refrigerator for 30 minutes, or chill them in the freezer for 15 minutes.

3. Meanwhile, preheat the oven to 350°F. Remove the cookies from the refrigerator and bake for 10 minutes until golden-brown at the edges. Cool slightly on the baking sheets, then transfer the cookies to a wire rack and let cool completely.

4. For the icing, sift the royal icing mix into a large bowl. Add 2 teaspoons cold water and, using an electric hand mixer, whisk on a low speed for 3 minutes until you have a smooth icing that holds soft peaks. Cover the bowl with a damp cloth or plastic wrap to prevent the icing from drying out.

5. Once the cookies are cold, spoon 5 tablespoons of the icing into a pastry bag fitted with the tip—you can just snip a small ⅛-inch tip off the end but a piping tip gives you more control. Pipe the white sections by tracing the inner edge of the base of the heart and drawing a wiggly line across the center.

6. Spoon one-third of the icing into a bowl and add ½ teaspoon water at a time to make flood icing—a thick, runny icing that smooths out on its own within 15 seconds. Fill the outlines with the runny icing. Divide the remaining icing into five bowls and

stir a little food coloring paste into each of them. Spoon some of each icing into separate pastry bags fitted with a ⅛-inch tip or just snip off the tip to make a small ⅛-inch hole. Using the different icings, pipe a line around the inner edge of the top of the hearts joining them to the edges of the white piping. You will get six of each colored cookie.

7. Once all the cookies have been outlined add a little water to each of the colored icings and fill in the hearts. Carefully scatter the tops with rainbow sprinkles and let set hard somewhere cool (but not the refrigerator) for at least 4 hours.

STAINED GLASS GINGERBREAD COOKIES

MAKES 35   PREP TIME: 40 MINUTES, PLUS COOLING, CHILLING, AND FREEZING   COOK TIME: 6 TO 10 MINUTES

Tie these spicy cookies with pretty colored ribbon or raffia and hang them on trees or in windows, so the sun can light up their rainbow centers.

2¾oz/scant ¼ cup light corn syrup or clear honey
3½oz/½ cup soft light brown sugar
3½oz/½ cup/1 stick unsalted butter
zest of ½ lemon
2 teaspoons ground ginger
1 teaspoon ground cinnamon
¼ teaspoon ground nutmeg
⅛ teaspoon ground cloves
½ teaspoon baking soda
10½oz/2¼ cups all-purpose flour, sifted, plus extra for dusting
1 medium egg, lightly beaten
5½ to 7oz fruit-flavored hard candies in different colors—each color crushed separately

YOU WILL NEED

Christmas-themed cutter(s) of your choice
smaller round or other shaped cutters
drinking straw
rainbow-colored ribbon or raffia

1. Place the syrup or honey, sugar, butter, lemon zest, and ground spices in a large, heavy-based saucepan and melt over a low-medium heat, stirring frequently, until the sugar has dissolved. Increase the heat and bring the mixture to a boil, then remove from the heat and beat in the baking soda. The mixture will froth up at this point as the baking soda reacts, so stir it briefly, then set aside to cool for 15 minutes.

2. Fold the flour into the melted mixture in batches, using a wooden spoon or a stand mixer. Finally, beat in the egg until combined. The dough will be sticky, but scrape it out of the bowl onto a very lightly floured surface and knead until smooth. Wrap in plastic wrap and chill in the refrigerator for 1 hour.

3. Preheat the oven to 350°F. Line three large baking sheets with parchment paper.

4. Roll out the gingerbread dough on a large sheet of wax paper to ⅛-inch thickness. Using the cutter(s) of your choice, cut out the dough (re-rolling any scraps) and then use an offset spatula to transfer them to the baking sheets. Leave space between each one for them to spread a little. Cut out small rounds or other shapes in the center of each cookie, making sure you leave a good border around the edge.

5. Using the end of a drinking straw, press it into the top of each cookie where you would like to thread a ribbon or raffia to hang it, then twist the straw and pull away to remove a tiny circle of dough. Alternatively, use a skewer to make the holes. Place the baking sheets in the freezer for 10 minutes.

6. Remove from the freezer, then fill the hole in the center of each cookie (not the one for the ribbon!) with a small pile of crushed hard candies.

7. Bake for 6 to 10 minutes, depending on size, until golden-brown at the edges Once cooked, check the hanging holes are still large enough to thread ribbon through; if not, use a skewer or the tip of a sharp knife to increase the size slightly.

8. Let the cookies cool on the baking sheets until the hard candies have hardened, then transfer them to a wire rack to cool completely. Once cold (after about 2 hours), tie each cookie with rainbow-colored ribbons or raffia, ready to hang.

ROCKY ROAD

SERVES 16   PREP TIME: 15 MINUTES   COOK TIME: 5 TO 10 MINUTES

The king of all rocky road! Intensely chocolatey and jam-packed with treats—this is definitely one to be enjoyed on a special occasion.

9oz/1 cup/2¼ sticks unsalted butter, plus extra for greasing
21oz dark chocolate (minimum 70% cocoa solids), roughly chopped
3 tablespoons light corn syrup
5½oz plain sandwich cookies
3oz pink wafers, halved
5½oz colored marshmallows
3½oz honeycomb, broken into pieces
5oz Crispy M&M's
1 teaspoon rainbow sprinkles/ nonpareils

1. Grease and line an 8-inch square cake pan with parchment paper. Melt the butter, chocolate, and syrup together in a medium, heavy-based pan over a low heat, stirring until smooth and combined. Set aside to cool a little.

2. Pour a ½-inch layer of the chocolate mixture over the base of the prepared pan. Scatter half of each of the cookies, marshmallows, honeycomb, and M&M's over the base. Pour over half the remaining chocolate mixture, then shake the pan a little to allow the chocolate to fill the holes.

3. Make a second layer with the remaining cookies, marshmallows, honeycomb, and M&M's (reserving a few to scatter over the top), then pour over the remaining chocolate mixture. Shake the pan as before to encourage the chocolate into any holes.

4. Scatter with the reserved ingredients, then finally scatter over the rainbow sprinkles. Let set somewhere cool (or the refrigerator) for at least 4 hours, before cutting into squares.

● ● ● ● ● ● ● ● ● ● ● ● ● ●

SWAP IN YOUR FAVORITE COOKIES OR CANDIES—JUST STICK TO THE QUANTITIES ABOVE SO IT SETS AND HOLDS TOGETHER WELL.

● ● ● ● ● ● ● ● ● ● ● ● ● ●

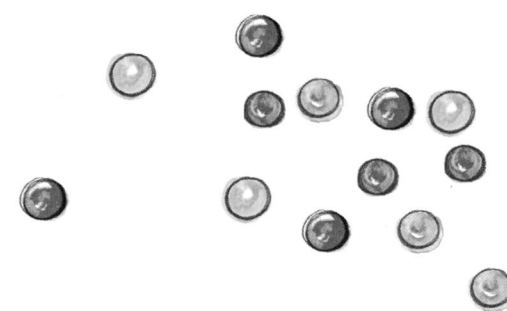

MULTICOLORED MACARONS

MAKES 28   PREP TIME: 25 MINUTES, PLUS 30 MINUTES RESTING AND COOLING   COOK TIME: 10 TO 12 MINUTES

Who can resist a macaron, especially when they come in a color medley!

9oz/2½ cups ground almonds
12oz/2½ cups powdered sugar
6 large egg whites
6oz/generous ¾ cup superfine sugar
2¾oz/⅓ cup/¾ stick salted butter, softened
food coloring pastes (purple, blue, green, yellow, orange, and pink)
2 tablespoons rainbow sprinkles/ nonpareils

FOR THE BUTTERCREAM

8oz/1 cup/2 sticks salted butter, softened
5½oz/1 cup powdered sugar
food coloring pastes (see above)

YOU WILL NEED

11 disposable pastry bags

MACARONS ARE VERY VULNERABLE TO HUMIDITY AND SMELLS, SO STORE THE SANDWICHED PAIRS IN AN AIRTIGHT CONTAINER IN THE REFRIGERATOR FOR UP TO 7 DAYS. STACK THEM CAREFULLY, WITH WAX PAPER BETWEEN EACH LAYER.

1. Line three baking sheets with parchment paper. Whizz the ground almonds and powdered sugar together in a food-processor until fine. Set aside.

2. Using an electric hand mixer, whisk the egg whites in a large, grease-free bowl until soft peaks form, then gradually whisk in the superfine sugar until glossy. Sift the almond mix over the egg whites and gently fold through with a large metal spoon.

3. Divide the mixture between seven bowls, then add a little food coloring paste to six of the bowls, gently folding it through evenly, then fold the rainbow sprinkles through the remaining bowl. Be very gentle when folding, so the mixtures don't become too loose or runny and therefore difficult to pipe.

4. Spoon one portion of colored mixture into a pastry bag and snip off the tip to make a ½-inch opening. Pipe 1 inch rounds onto the baking sheets (each batch of mixture will make about 8 macarons). Repeat with the remaining colored mixtures and the sprinkles mixture, using a fresh pastry bag each time.

5. Tap the baking sheets twice on the work surface to flatten out the macarons and to dislodge any air bubbles. If any peaks are left, lightly wet a finger and gently dab the peak flat. Set aside to rest for 30 minutes, or until the macarons have formed a skin on the surface when you lightly touch them.

6. Meanwhile, preheat the oven to 300°F. Bake the macarons for 10 to 12 minutes, then let cool.

7. For the buttercream, beat the butter and powdered sugar together in a small bowl until light and fluffy. Divide between four bowls and add a little food coloring paste to each portion. Spoon each into a separate pastry bag, then snip off the tip of each bag to make a ½-inch opening. Pipe some buttercream onto the bases of an alternate color macaron, then sandwich them together with a different colored macaron on top.

FLOWER COOKIES

MAKES 28   PREP TIME: 45 MINUTES, PLUS CHILLING AND COOLING   COOK TIME: 10-12 MINUTES

Get your pastry bags at the ready! These bright flower cookies are super simple to make and elegant too, providing a perfect gift for Mother's Day.

7oz/¾/1¾ sticks unsalted butter,
  softened
7oz/1 cup superfine sugar
zest of 1 orange
1 large egg, lightly beaten
14oz/3 cups all-purpose flour,
  plus extra for dusting

FOR THE BUTTERCREAM

9oz/1 cup/2¼ sticks unsalted butter,
  softened
18oz/3½ cups powdered sugar,
  sifted
food coloring pastes (blue, green,
  yellow, orange, and pink)

YOU WILL NEED

3-inch round cookie cutter
5 disposable pastry bags
¾-inch closed star tip

1. Using an electric hand mixer, beat the butter, superfine sugar, and orange zest together in a medium bowl until just combined and becoming creamy (don't overwork, otherwise the cookies will spread during baking). Add the egg and beat until combined. Sift in the flour and stir gently until the mixture comes together to form a dough. Shape into a ball, then cut in half and wrap each portion in plastic wrap. Chill in the refrigerator for 1 hour.

2. Line two or three large baking sheets with parchment paper, then set aside. On a lightly floured surface, roll out the dough to ⅛-inch thickness. Using the cookie cutter, cut out 28 cookies, then transfer them to the prepared baking sheets. Chill in the refrigerator again for 30 minutes, or speed things up by chilling them in the freezer for 15 minutes.

3. Meanwhile, preheat the oven to 350°F. Remove the cookies from the refrigerator and bake for 10 to 12 minutes until golden-brown at the edges. Cool for 5 minutes on the baking sheets, then transfer to a wire rack and let cool completely.

4. For the buttercream, beat the butter and sugar together in a bowl until light and fluffy. Divide between five smaller bowls and stir a little food coloring paste into each portion.

5. Spoon one of the icings into a pastry bag fitted with the tip and pipe swirls from the center working outward, gradually tapering them off so they look like roses. Wash the tip and insert into a clean pastry bag, then fill with another colored icing to continue piping flowers onto the cookies. Repeat this process with the remaining icings. Let set, uncovered, in a cool place for 2 to 3 hours.

COOKIE CAKE

SERVES 10　PREP TIME: 20 MINUTES, PLUS COOLING　COOK TIME: 25-30 MINUTES

Looking for something a little different to celebrate someone's birthday? This soft giant cookie cake studded with a rainbow of chocolates is bound to put a smile on anybody's face.

4½oz/½ cup/1⅛ sticks unsalted butter, softened, plus extra for greasing

2¾oz/⅓ cup soft light brown sugar

2¾oz/⅓ cup granulated sugar

1 medium egg

1 teaspoon vanilla extract

8oz/1¾ cups all-purpose flour, plus extra for dusting

½ teaspoon baking powder

1 teaspoon baking soda

½ teaspoon fine salt

3½oz hazelnuts or macadamia nuts, roughly chopped

4½oz dark chocolate (minimum 70% cocoa solids), roughly chopped

6oz Peanut M&M's or other flavored M&M's

1. Preheat the oven to 350°F. Grease an 8½-inch loose-based cake pan, then lightly dust with flour to coat.

2. Using an electric hand mixer, beat the butter and sugars together in a medium bowl until light and fluffy. Add the egg and vanilla extract and beat again to combine. Sift in the flour, baking powder, baking soda, and salt, then fold into the mixture until just combined.

3. Stir through three-quarters of each of the nuts, chocolate chunks, and M&M's, then press the mixture evenly into the prepared pan. Scatter with the remaining nuts, chocolate, and M&M's and press into the dough slightly.

4. Bake for 25 to 30 minutes until golden and puffed. Cover with foil after 15 minutes if it is beginning to brown too quickly. Let cool completely in the pan before removing and slicing into wedges to serve.

CANDIES & DESSERTS

RAINBOW FUDGE

MAKES 60 PIECES   PREP TIME: 30 MINUTES, PLUS FREEZING AND CHILLING   COOK TIME: 5 TO 10 MINUTES

This is the simplest cheat's fudge you will ever make—there is no boiling involved, so it is safe and fun to make with children.

vegetable or sunflower oil,
  for greasing
1lb good-quality white chocolate
  (minimum 30% cocoa solids),
  roughly chopped
14oz can condensed milk
1¼oz salted butter
½ teaspoon orange extract
food coloring pastes (purple, blue,
  green, yellow, orange, and red)

1. Lightly grease an 8½ × 4½ × 2½-inch loaf pan with a little oil and line with plastic wrap.

2. Place the white chocolate, condensed milk, and butter in a medium, heavy-based saucepan and set it over a low-medium heat. Stir gently until melted, smooth, and combined, then stir in the orange extract.

3. Divide between six bowls and stir a little food coloring paste into each portion until well combined.

4. Pour the purple mixture into the lined loaf pan and freeze for 15 minutes. Meanwhile, cover the remaining bowls with plastic wrap. Repeat this process with the blue, green, yellow, orange, and red mixtures, pouring each mixture over the previous layer and freezing each layer as above. Cover with plastic wrap and let set overnight in the refrigerator until firm.

5. Turn out onto a chopping board, peel off the plastic wrap and cut the fudge into 20 even slices, then cut each slice into three pieces. Store in an airtight container in the refrigerator to keep the fudge nice and firm.

PACKED INTO AN AIRTIGHT CONTAINER (WITH PARCHMENT PAPER BETWEEN EACH LAYER) AND STORED IN THE REFRIGERATOR, THIS FUDGE WILL KEEP WELL FOR UP TO 2 WEEKS.

RAINBOW UNICORN BALLS

MAKES 28   PREP TIME: 40 MINUTES, PLUS COOLING, FREEZING, SETTING, AND CHILLING   COOK TIME: 15 MINUTES

These truffles are great as gifts and for sharing with friends.

6fl oz/⅔ cup whipping cream
pinch of salt
2¾oz/⅓ cup granulated sugar
4½oz/½ cup/1⅛ sticks unsalted
   butter, softened
2 tablespoons rainbow sprinkles/
   nonpareils

TO COAT AND DECORATE

5½oz good-quality dark chocolate
   (minimum 70% cocoa solids),
   roughly chopped
5½oz good-quality white chocolate
   (minimum 30% cocoa solids),
   roughly chopped
2 teaspoons peanut, almond,
   or walnut oil
3 tablespoons rainbow sprinkles/
   nonpareils

YOU WILL NEED

large pastry bag fitted with a large
round tip

● ● ● ● ● ● ● ● ● ● ● ● ● ● ●

**FOR ADDED FLAVOR, USE FLAVORED
CHOCOLATE OR STIR IN 1 TABLESPOON OF
YOUR FAVORITE LIQUEUR OR 1 TEASPOON
OF ORANGE OR PEPPERMINT EXTRACT
WHEN YOU STIR THE SUGAR
INTO THE MIXTURE IN STEP 1.**

● ● ● ● ● ● ● ● ● ● ● ● ● ● ●

1. Line two baking sheets with parchment paper and set aside. Pour the whipping cream into a saucepan and add the salt. Set over a low heat and bring to just below boiling point. Remove from the heat and stir in the sugar until dissolved. Set aside to cool to 68°F (room temperature).

2. Using an electric hand mixer, beat the butter in a medium bowl until light and fluffy. Gradually pour in the cream mixture, beating continuously until smooth and combined. (If the mixture curdles, it is too cold, but you can rescue it by gently heating the bowl in a water bath until it re-emulsifies. If your mixture is too runny, place the bowl in a bowl of iced water and whisk until it thickens.) Add the sprinkles and stir to combine.

3. Spoon the truffle mixture into the pastry bag and then pipe neat walnut-sized rounds onto your prepared baking sheets. Transfer the trays to the freezer and let set for 1 hour.

4. Meanwhile, place each type of chocolate in a separate heatproof bowl and add 1 teaspoon of the oil to each. Set one bowl over a pan of barely simmering water, making sure the base of the bowl doesn't touch the water, and leave for about 5 minutes until the chocolate is melted and smooth, stirring once or twice. Repeat with the other bowl of chocolate. Remove from the heat and set aside to cool to 104°F (hand-hot).

5. Once the truffle centers are ready, dip them, one at a time, into the melted chocolates (dipping half of them into the dark chocolate and the remainder into the white chocolate). Lift each truffle out by scooping it up with a fork and allowing the excess chocolate to dribble off back into the bowl. Place the truffles back on the lined baking sheets, then scatter with the sprinkles. Place in the refrigerator for 1 hour to set before serving. These truffles will keep well the refrigerator, in an airtight container (with parchment paper between each layer) for 2 weeks.

FRUIT JELLIES

MAKES 30 JELLIES OF YOUR CHOSEN FLAVOR   PREP TIME: 30 MINUTES, PLUS COOLING AND SETTING
COOK TIME: 15 TO 25 MINUTES

Bursting with natural fruits, these jellies are packed with tangy flavor.

vegetable oil, for greasing

14 to 18oz prepared fruit for one
  flavor (see flavors, below)

10½oz/1½ cups superfine sugar

2 tablespoons lemon juice

3 tablespoons apple-based
  liquid pectin

5½oz/¾ cup granulated sugar

FOR PINEAPPLE FLAVOR

14oz chopped pineapple flesh, plus
  a little yellow food coloring paste

FOR BLACKBERRY FLAVOR

14oz blackberries

FOR STRAWBERRY FLAVOR

14oz hulled and quartered
  strawberries

FOR MANDARIN FLAVOR

14oz drained, canned
  mandarin segments

FOR KIWI FLAVOR

18oz peeled and chopped
  kiwi fruit, plus a little green
  food coloring paste

YOU WILL NEED

candy thermometer

1. Lightly grease a loaf pan and line with plastic wrap, making sure it goes right up the sides and into the corners of the pan.

2. Whizz your chosen fruit in a small blender until smooth. Press through a fine strainer to remove any pith or seeds. Transfer the fruit puree (which will now be about 10½oz) to a heavy-based saucepan and add the superfine sugar. Place over a low heat and stir gently until the sugar has dissolved.

3. Gradually increase the heat, stirring constantly so the mixture doesn't catch and burn, until it reaches 225°F on a candy thermometer. This will take between 10 to 20 minutes (be careful as some fruits have a higher pectin content than others, so some will reach the temperature and thicken more quickly).

4. Add the lemon juice and pectin and stir to combine, then reheat until the mixture again reaches a temperature of 225°F (setting point) and it is thick and like a soft jam. (To test this, get a small bowl of cold chilled water and drop half a teaspoon of the mixture into it. It should hold together and set in a small ball. If not, return the pan to the heat and continue to cook for a further few minutes before testing again.) Once the mixture has reached setting point, stir in the food coloring paste (if using), then pour into the lined pan and let cool. Cover with plastic wrap and let set somewhere cool or in the refrigerator overnight.

5. Pour the granulated sugar into a baking sheet. Turn the fruit jelly block out onto the sugar and gently peel off the plastic wrap. Run a large sharp knife under a hot tap then wipe dry and cut the jelly block into cubes, then gently turn them in the sugar to coat. Let set, uncovered, for 1 hour before serving. Packed into an airtight container, with parchment paper between each layer, they will keep in a cool, dry place for up to 3 weeks.

RAINBOW BARK

SERVES 8   PREP TIME: 15 MINUTES, PLUS SETTING AND CHILLING   COOK TIME: 10 MINUTES

This beautiful natural rainbow, made from mixed dried fruits and nuts, makes a simple chocolate treat something much more special. Great for Father's Day and so simple that the kids can make it by themselves.

18oz dark chocolate (minimum 70% cocoa solids), roughly chopped
1¾oz white chocolate (minimum 30% cocoa solids), roughly chopped
¼oz whole freeze-dried raspberries
1¾oz dried banana chips
¼oz dried mango, cut into strips
¼oz pistachios, roughly chopped
¼oz dried coconut flakes

1. Line a 10 × 15-inch jelly roll pan with parchment paper and set aside.

2. Place each chocolate in a separate heatproof bowl. Set one bowl over a pan of barely simmering water, making sure the base of the bowl doesn't touch the water, and leave for about 5 minutes until the chocolate is melted and smooth, stirring once or twice. Repeat with the other bowl of chocolate. Remove from the heat.

3. Pour the melted dark chocolate into the prepared pan and let cool slightly at room temperature, about 5 minutes. Place spoonfuls of the melted white chocolate randomly over the dark chocolate and then use a skewer or the tip of a sharp knife to marble the chocolates together.

4. Leave again at room temperature for 5 to 10 minutes until set slightly but still soft, then scatter over the raspberries, banana, mango, pistachios, and coconut flakes.

5. Transfer to the refrigerator and let set hard for 2 hours. Once set, turn out of the pan and break up roughly into shards. Stored in an airtight container, somewhere cool, this bark will keep well for up to 2 weeks.

SCATTER WITH ANY OF YOUR FAVORITE DRIED FRUITS AND NUTS. YOU CAN EVEN FINISH OFF WITH A SPRINKLE OF SEA SALT OR CHILI FLAKES FOR A LITTLE KICK!

RAINBOW MERINGUES

MAKES 40   PREP TIME: 30 MINUTES   COOK TIME: 30 TO 35 MINUTES

Soft, chewy, and small enough to pop a few in your mouth without anyone seeing! These pretty little meringues make the perfect gift.

2 medium egg whites (about 2oz)
about 4½oz/generous ½ cup
  superfine sugar (double the
  weight of the egg whites)
½ teaspoon vanilla extract
¼ teaspoon fine salt
food coloring pastes (purple, blue,
  green, yellow, orange, and pink)

YOU WILL NEED

long fine paintbrush
large disposable pastry bag fitted
  with a ½-inch round tip

● ● ● ● ● ● ● ● ● ● ● ● ● ●

**USE A PAPER TOWEL AND A LITTLE
WHITE WINE VINEGAR TO CLEAN YOUR
BOWL AND WHISK ATTACHMENTS
BEFORE WHISKING THE EGG WHITES
TO ENSURE EVERYTHING IS GREASE
FREE, ALLOWING THE EGG WHITES
TO WHISK UP WELL.**

● ● ● ● ● ● ● ● ● ● ● ● ● ●

1. Preheat the oven to 250°F. Line two or three baking sheets with parchment paper.

2. Using an electric hand mixer, whisk the egg whites in a medium, grease-free bowl, starting with a low speed and gradually increasing it to high, until stiff peaks form. Begin to add the sugar, a tablespoon at a time, whisking well after each addition, until all the sugar is incorporated. Whisk the mixture for a further 5 minutes to completely dissolve all the sugar. You can check this by rubbing a little meringue mixture between your fingers to make sure no grains remain. If it's still grainy, continue to whisk a little more.

3. Once the meringue is smooth and glossy, whisk in the vanilla extract and salt.

4. Take the pastry bag and turn the top down about halfway. Using the paintbrush, draw lines of food coloring paste on the inside of the bag all the way up from the tip end to the wider open top of the bag. For pastel shades use a thin line of paste, and for more intense colors use a thicker line of paste. Remember to clean the brush between applying each color.

5. Once you have drawn all the colored lines on the inside of the pastry bag, carefully add spoonfuls of meringue to the bag, starting as low down in the bag as you can. Make sure the bag doesn't collapse and spread the colors. Gently pull the sides of the bag back up and twist the top to secure. (You can place the bag in a measuring pitcher and fold the top of the bag down over the sides, then add the colors and meringue. This keeps the bag in place and avoids any slippages.)

6. Pipe small teardrops onto the prepared baking sheets, leaving about 2 inches between each one. Bake for 30 to 35 minutes. When the meringues are ready, they will pull off the paper easily—if they don't, pop them back in for a few more minutes until they are ready. Set aside to cool on the baking sheets for 1 hour, then peel off the paper. Serve or store. Stored in an airtight container (with parchment paper between each layer), these meringues will keep well, in a cool, dry place, for up to 2 weeks.

FRUIT ROLLS

MAKES 10 ROLLS OF YOUR CHOSEN FLAVOR   PREP TIME: 15 MINUTES   COOK TIME: 8-10 HOURS

These healthy snacks are a real hit with kids and make a great swap for sweets in lunch boxes.

FOR THE RASPBERRY AND ROSEWATER FLAVOR

7oz raspberries
¼ teaspoon rosewater
1 tablespoon superfine sugar
  or honey

FOR THE BLACKBERRY AND MINT FLAVOR

7oz blackberries
juice of ½ lime
10 mint leaves
1 tablespoon superfine sugar
  or honey

FOR THE PLUM AND VANILLA FLAVOR

7oz (prepared weight) plums, pitted
  and chopped
¼ teaspoon vanilla extract
1 tablespoon superfine sugar
  or honey

FOR THE MANGO AND LIME FLAVOR

7oz (prepared weight) fresh mango,
  peeled, pitted, and chopped
juice of ½ lime
1 tablespoon superfine sugar
  or honey

FOR THE STRAWBERRY FLAVOR

7oz (prepared weight) strawberries,
  hulled and halved
1 tablespoon superfine sugar
  or honey

1. Preheat the oven to 140°F. If you use an electric fan oven, then the fruit dries out much more quickly and can cause the fruit rolls to crack, so in these cases, preheat the oven to its lowest temperature and check the fruit rolls after just half the cooking time given below. Line a baking sheet, about 10 × 14 inches, with parchment paper.

2. Choose your flavor, then wash and prepare the fruit. Put the fruit in a blender with the other flavorings listed for each one (if applicable), along with the sugar or honey. Whizz to a smooth puree. Pour the mixture into the lined baking sheet and tilt it to spread the puree out evenly.

3. Bake for 8 to 10 hours or overnight until dry to touch. Remove from the oven and let cool completely on the baking sheet. Once cold, peel off the lining paper, then cut the fruit mixture into strips and roll up. Stored in an airtight container (with parchment paper between each layer), these fruit rolls will keep well in a cool, dry place for up to 3 weeks.

• •

YOU CAN BAKE UP TO THREE BATCHES OF FRUIT ROLLS AT THE SAME TIME—MAKE ONE BATCH AFTER THE OTHER AND POP EACH ONE INTO THE OVEN AS YOU GO. ABOUT HALFWAY THROUGH, SWAP THE POSITION OF THE TRAYS AROUND.

IF YOU WANT TO LIVEN UP THE COLOR OF THE FRUIT PUREES, SIMPLY STIR A LITTLE FOOD COLORING PASTE INTO THE PUREE BEFORE POURING IT ONTO THE BAKING SHEET TO BAKE.

• •

RAINBOW CREPE CAKE WITH WHITE CHOCOLATE GANACHE

SERVES 12   PREP TIME: 30 MINUTES, PLUS CHILLING AND COOLING   COOK TIME: 1¼ HOURS

For those who just aren't into cake (I know, crazy right?!) or are just looking for something a little bit different, this impressive crepe tower will hit the spot perfectly.

FOR THE WHIPPED CHOCOLATE GANACHE

25fl oz/3¼ cups heavy cream
1lb white chocolate (minimum 30% cocoa solids), finely chopped

FOR THE CREPES

1½ quarts/6 cups whole milk
6oz/¾ cup/1½ sticks unsalted butter, plus extra for greasing
12 large eggs
14oz/3 cups all-purpose flour
4½oz/generous ½ cup superfine sugar
½ teaspoon salt
zest of 2 oranges
food coloring pastes (purple, blue, green, yellow, orange, and red)
1 tablespoon powdered sugar, to dust
1 tablespoon edible gold stars

1. First make the whipped chocolate ganache. Pour the cream into a medium saucepan over a low heat and bring to just below boiling point. Remove from the heat, add the chopped chocolate, and let melt for 1 minute, then stir gently until smooth and combined. Pour into a bowl and let cool, then cover and chill in the refrigerator for at least 2 hours until firm. Once chilled, beat with an electric hand mixer until soft peaks form.

2. Once the ganache is chilling, you can make the crepes. Heat the milk in a medium, heavy-based saucepan until small bubbles appear at the edges. Meanwhile, melt the butter in a separate pan. Set both aside and let cool slightly.

3. Using a stand mixer with a whisk attachment, or an electric hand mixer, whisk the eggs, flour, superfine sugar, salt, and orange zest together until combined. Reduce to a low speed and then gradually add the butter and milk until incorporated.

4. Divide the batter between six bowls and stir a little food coloring paste into each portion.

5. Heat two large (8½-inch diameter) skillets over a low-medium heat and grease each one with a little butter. Pour a few tablespoons of the first colored batter into each pan and swirl each to coat the pan evenly. Cook for 1 to 2 minutes until the edges begin to brown, then flip the crepes and cook for an additional 1 to 1½ minutes. Remove the cooked crepes to a large plate and place a sheet of wax paper in between each

TO MAKE THE BATTER IN ADVANCE, FOLLOW STEPS 2 AND 3, THEN COVER AND CHILL IN THE REFRIGERATOR FOR UP TO 24 HOURS. WHISK THE BATTER, THEN DIVIDE AND COLOR AS ABOVE, BEFORE COOKING THE CREPES. ALTERNATIVELY, YOU CAN MAKE AND COOL THE CREPES AS ABOVE, THEN COVER THEM WITH PLASTIC WRAP AND CHILL IN THE REFRIGERATOR FOR UP TO 24 HOURS.

one. Repeat (greasing the pans between each use) until all the colored batters are used up, stacking the crepes as you go. Set the cooked crepes aside and let cool completely.

6. To assemble, stack the colored crepes on top of each other, spreading a thin layer of the whipped chocolate ganache between each one, working your way through the colors of the rainbow as you stack. Once assembled, chill the crepe cake in the refrigerator for 2 hours, then dust with powdered sugar and edible gold stars just before serving. Cut into wedges to serve.

MARBLED MARSHMALLOWS

**MAKES 48 MARSHMALLOWS OF YOUR 2 CHOSEN FLAVORS   PREP TIME: 50 MINUTES, PLUS COOLING AND SETTING
COOK TIME: 15 MINUTES**

You haven't experienced a marshmallow until you have tried a home-made one. Billowy and white, they are the perfect sweet treat to flavor and color, to create a rainbow of irresistible, lighter-than-air marshmallows.

1 teaspoon sunflower oil
1¼oz/3½ tablespoons powdered sugar
1¼oz/3½ tablespoons cornstarch
½oz (about 8 to 9 sheets) leaf gelatin
18oz/2½ cups granulated sugar
1 tablespoon glucose syrup
2 large egg whites
food coloring pastes of your choice to match the flavorings (optional)

FOR THE FLAVORS

Pineapple and lime
14oz chopped pineapple flesh
1 tablespoon granulated sugar
zest and juice of ½ lime

Blackberry and mint
12oz blackberries
1 tablespoon granulated sugar
juice of ½ lemon
sprig of fresh mint, leaves picked and finely chopped

Raspberry
12oz raspberries
1 tablespoon granulated sugar
juice of ½ lemon

Pistachio
2¾oz pistachios, roughly chopped
green food coloring paste

1. Choose two flavors and place the ingredients for each (except with the pistachio one) into separate medium, heavy-based saucepans and set over a medium heat. Bring to a boil, then simmer for 5 to 10 minutes, stirring frequently, until thick and jammy. Cool slightly, then press the mixture through a fine strainer to remove any seeds and excess pulp. Set aside to cool slightly.

2. Grease an 8 × 12-inch rectangle cake pan with the sunflower oil. Sift the powdered sugar and cornstarch together in a small bowl, then dust the pan with the mixture, tapping it over the base and up the sides to create an even coating. Tap out any excess into a small bowl, then cover and reserve.

3. Place the gelatin leaves in a shallow bowl of cold water and set aside.

4. Place the granulated sugar, glucose syrup and 1 cup of cold water in a medium, heavy-based saucepan over a low heat. Stir frequently until the sugar has dissolved, then insert a candy thermometer and increase the heat. Bring the sugar syrup up to a temperature of 262°F, without stirring, then remove from the heat.

5. Using an electric hand mixer, whisk the egg whites in a large, grease-free bowl until stiff peaks form. Once the sugar syrup is ready, continue whisking the egg whites on a low speed whilst carefully pouring the hot sugar syrup down the inside edge of the bowl.

6. Gently squeeze the excess liquid out of the soaked gelatin, then add the gelatin to the egg white mixture. Gradually increase the whisking speed to high, continuing until the

●●●●●●●●●●●●●●●●

PACKED INTO AN AIRTIGHT CONTAINER (LAYERED BETWEEN SHEETS OF PARCHMENT PAPER) AND STORED IN A COOL, DRY PLACE, THE MARSHMALLOWS WILL KEEP WELL FOR UP TO A MONTH.

●●●●●●●●●●●●●●●●

mixture is thick and holds its shape on the whisk when you lift it out. It will have doubled in size.

7. Transfer half of the egg white mixture into another bowl, then fold your two cooled flavored pulps through one portion each to gently marble. At this point you can add a little food coloring paste if you want a more vibrant color. If you are making the pistachio flavor, just fold the nuts through the egg white mixture now along with a little green food coloring paste.

8. Tilting the prepared pan, spoon one of the mixtures into one side of the pan, then place the pan flat and quickly spoon in the other flavor so the two flavors meet in the middle. Smooth the surface with a wet spatula. Tightly cover the pan with plastic wrap, ensuring the plastic wrap doesn't touch the marshmallow mixture, then set aside somewhere cool (but not the refrigerator) for at least 4 hours or overnight.

9. Once set, dust a chopping board with the reserved powdered sugar and cornstarch mixture. Pass a knife all around the edge of the marshmallow to loosen it and turn out onto the board. Cut into squares with a wet sharp knife, cleaning the knife after every few slices. Roll each square in the powdered sugar and cornstarch mixture to coat. Serve or store.

FRUIT SORBET ICE CREAM CAKE

SERVES 16   PREP TIME: 1 TO 1¼ HOURS, PLUS FREEZING

This is soon to be your new favorite dessert! Treat friends to a slice
of wonderful, tasty rainbow flavors and colors.

18fl oz/2 cups strawberry sorbet

18fl oz/2 cups mango sorbet

18fl oz/2 cups blueberry frozen
yogurt

18fl oz/2 cups lemon sorbet

18fl oz/2 cups raspberry sorbet

18fl oz/2 cups pistachio ice cream

FOR THE WHIPPED CREAM ICING

14fl oz/1¾ cups whipping cream

1¾oz/⅓ cup powdered sugar, sifted

½ teaspoon vanilla extract

TO DECORATE

9oz mixed frozen fruit

1. Line a 9-inch loose-based round cake pan with two layers of
   plastic wrap. Remove the first sorbet from the freezer and remove
   all the packaging. Cut the sorbet into slices and press into the
   lined pan with the back of a large spoon, spreading it level. Place
   in the freezer and leave for 1½ to 2 hours, or until set hard.

2. Repeat with the next sorbet, pressing the slices in an even layer
   over the first sorbet layer, then freeze again, as above. Continue
   in the same way with the remaining sorbets, frozen yogurt, and
   ice cream, freezing each layer as before (you can choose if you
   would like the layers to be in the order of a traditional rainbow
   or if you prefer a more random theme to your colored layers).

3. Once they are all used up and layered on top of each other,
   cover the whole pan with plastic wrap and freeze for several
   hours or overnight until firm (the dessert can now stay in the
   freezer until you are ready to serve).

4. When you are ready to serve the sorbet cake, remove it
   from the freezer, uncover, and carefully release it from the
   tin, peeling off the plastic wrap. Place it on a serving plate
   and return to the freezer for 30 minutes to set the surface.

5. Meanwhile, for the whipped cream icing, using an electric
   hand mixer, whip the cream in a medium bowl until soft peaks
   form, then whisk in the powdered sugar and vanilla extract
   until combined. Immediately spread the icing over the frozen
   cake with an offset spatula. Return the cake to the freezer for a
   further 15 minutes to firm up, then remove and scatter with the
   frozen fruit. Cut into wedges to serve.

MARBLED CHEESECAKE

What better way to end a meal than with this rainbow-swirled, creamy vanilla cheesecake with a crunchy ginger cookie base?

½ teaspoon vegetable oil

12oz ginger cookies

4½oz/½ cup/1⅛ sticks unsalted butter, melted

36oz/4 cups full-fat cream cheese, at room temperature

9oz/1¼ cups granulated sugar

4 large eggs, lightly beaten

8fl oz/1 cup sour cream

1 teaspoon vanilla extract

2 tablespoons cornstarch

food coloring pastes (blue, green, orange, and pink)

1. Preheat the oven to 325°F. Pour some water into a large, shallow roasting pan and place it in the bottom of the oven. Grease a 9-inch springform pan with the vegetable oil and line the base with parchment paper.

2. Whizz the cookies in a food-processor until you have fine crumbs. Transfer to a bowl and stir through the melted butter. Press into the base and up the sides of the pan using the back of a spoon to flatten it evenly. Bake for 10 minutes, then let cool completely.

3. Reduce the oven temperature to 250°F. Using an electric hand mixer, beat the cream cheese and sugar together in a large bowl until light and fluffy. Lightly beat in the eggs, a little at a time, until combined. Beat in the sour cream, vanilla extract, and cornstarch until smooth and combined.

4. Place one-third of the mixture in a bowl, then divide the remaining mixture between four bowls. Stir a little food coloring paste into each of the portions until well combined. Using a large spoon, alternately place the plain and colored mixtures over the cookie base. Use the tip of a sharp knife to gently swirl the colors together, creating a marbled effect.

5. Bake for 1½ hours, or until the filling is set but still jiggles slightly in the center when the pan is gently nudged. Turn the oven off and leave the cheesecake to cool completely inside before taking it out. Chill in the refrigerator for at least 3 to 4 hours or overnight before removing from the pan and serving in slices.

YOU CAN LAYER UP THE CHEESECAKE BATTER IN THE PAN AS AN ALTERNATIVE TO MARBLING IF YOU WISH.

RAINBOW OF FRUIT TART

SERVES 10   PREP TIME: 40 MINUTES, PLUS CHILLING AND COOLING   COOK TIME: 20 MINUTES

Liven up your dessert with a natural burst of color. This beautiful tart
is so easy to assemble and is bound to impress.

FOR THE PASTRY

3oz/⅓ cup/¾ stick unsalted
  butter, softened
2¼oz/generous ¼ cup
  superfine sugar
3 large egg yolks
7oz/1½ cups all-purpose flour,
  plus extra for dusting

FOR THE TOPPING

4½fl oz/½ cup heavy cream
4½oz mascarpone cheese
10½oz natural Greek yogurt
1¾oz/⅓ cup powdered sugar,
  sifted
1 teaspoon vanilla extract
21oz prepared and washed mixed
  fresh fruit (such as papaya,
  mango, kiwi, passion fruit,
  clementine segments, whole
  berries, and grapes), sliced or
  left whole as you wish
zest of 1 lime

YOU WILL NEED

baking beans or raw rice

1. Using an electric hand mixer, beat the butter and sugar together in a medium bowl until creamy, then beat in the egg yolks, one at a time, until combined. Sift over the flour and fold in until the mixture comes together to form a dough.

2. Tip the dough onto a lightly floured surface and knead briefly until smooth. Roll into a ball, then press gently into a disc, wrap in plastic wrap and chill in the refrigerator for 30 minutes.

3. Preheat the oven to 400°F. Roll out the pastry on a lightly floured surface to a 18 × 8½-inch rectangle, then use it to line a 14 × 4½-inch fluted rectangular tart pan (the pastry will hang over the edges of the pan, which is correct—you'll trim these to neaten later). Place on a baking sheet, then prick the base of the tart all over with a fork, line with wax paper and fill with baking beans or raw rice.

4. Bake for 15 minutes. Remove the paper and baking beans or rice and bake for a further 5 minutes. Remove from the oven and let cool completely on a wire rack. Trim off the excess pastry with a sharp knife to neaten the edges, then carefully remove from the pan and place the pastry shell on a serving plate.

5. Whip the cream in a bowl until soft peaks form, then whisk in the mascarpone, yogurt, powdered sugar, and vanilla extract. Spoon the cream mixture into the cold pastry shell, spreading it out with the back of a spoon and creating a few peaks.

6. Arrange the mixed fruit over the cream mixture, then scatter with the lime zest to decorate. Serve immediately.

INDEX

THANK YOUS

First, thank you to any one who has bought one of my books and has come back for more! Baking is such a passion of mine and I love to share my recipes with others who are looking for a bit of fun and inspiration in the kitchen.

To my creative rainbow book team! It is so inspiring to work with a group of people who constantly surprise you with new wonderful ideas of how to squeeze more color or a little joke onto a page. I've said it before but it really is true—though our jobs can be demanding they are always great fun! The delight and enthusiasm from everyone involved I believe shines through on the pages of this book and for that I am very grateful.

To Sophie, for always wanting more color, more rainbows, and more unicorns! Thank you for encouraging any kind of wackiness to help to make this book as playful as it was intended.

To Danielle, for your patience while rainbow masterpieces took time to create in the kitchen! For not being phased when increasingly more and more colorful bakes were put on set and for always managing to put together the perfect shot to show off each rainbow.

To Lauren and Lydia, for teaming up to make Rainbow Bakes as fun, colorful and stylish as I imagined it could be and for scouring London high and low for rainbows and unicorns galore!

To Louise, for pulling all our multi-colored magic together and making it something wonderful. You instantly got the essence of the book and, Sarah, your tubby unicorn will live in my dreams forever!

To Millicent and Ted, for beautiful hands, strong arms, and photographic skills that made our shoots breeze by.

To Amber, for washing and drying rainbow icing bowls over and over again with the knowledge that you wouldn't get to eat any of the cake!

To Bear, for the excruciating job of helping to clear up all the rainbow sprinkles that made it onto the floor.

And to Tom, this time for laughing at my rainbow icing stained feet when they poked out the end of the bed after a long, exhausting day recipe testing. For saying all the right things when sampling rainbow cake, and for carrying bags and boxes back and forth to the car for the photo shoots. You are my pot of gold at the end of the rainbow.